(De)constructing Societal Threats During Times of Deep Mediatization

This book explores how both elite and non-elite actors frame societal threats such as the refugee crisis and COVID-19 using both digital and traditional media. It also explores ways in which the framing of these issues as threatening can be challenged using these platforms.

People typically experience societal threats such as war and terrorism through the media they consume, both on and offline. Much of the research in this area to date focuses on either how political and media elites present these issues to citizens or audience responses to these frames. This book takes a different approach by focusing on how issues such as the refugee crisis and the COVID-19 pandemic are both constructed and deconstructed in an era of hybrid media. It draws on a range of traditional and innovative research methodologies to explore how these issues are framed as 'threats' within deeply mediatized societies, ranging from content analysis of newspaper coverage of the Macedonian name dispute in Greece to investigating conspiratorial communities on YouTube using Systemic Functional Linguistics. In doing so, this book enriches our understanding of not only how civil and uncivil actors frame these issues but also their impact on societal resilience towards future crises.

(De)constructing Societal Threats During Times of Deep Mediatization will be a key resource for academics, researchers, and advanced students of Communication Studies, Media Studies, Journalism, Cultural Studies, Research Methods, Sociology, and Politics. The chapters included in this book were originally published as a special issue of *The Communication Review*.

Paul Reilly is Senior Lecturer in Communications, Media and Democracy at the University of Glasgow, UK.

Virpi Salojärvi is Assistant Professor in Communication Studies at the University of Vaasa, Finland, and University Researcher at the Helsinki Hub on Emotions, Populism and Polarisation (HEPPsinki) at the University of Helsinki, Finland.

(De)constructing Societal Threats During Times of Deep Mediatization

Edited by
Paul Reilly and Virpi Salojärvi

NEW YORK AND LONDON

First published 2024
by Routledge
605 Third Avenue, New York, NY 10158

and by Routledge
4 Park Square, Milton Park, Abingdon, Oxon, OX14 4RN

Routledge is an imprint of the Taylor & Francis Group, an informa business

Introduction, Chapters 1–3 © 2024 Taylor & Francis
Chapter 4 © 2022 Gregory Asmolov. Originally published as Open Access.

With the exception of Chapter 4, no part of this book may be reprinted or reproduced or utilised in any form or by any electronic, mechanical, or other means, now known or hereafter invented, including photocopying and recording, or in any information storage or retrieval system, without permission in writing from the publishers. For details on the rights for Chapter 4, please see the chapter's Open Access footnote.

Trademark notice: Product or corporate names may be trademarks or registered trademarks, and are used only for identification and explanation without intent to infringe.

British Library Cataloguing-in-Publication Data
A catalogue record for this book is available from the British Library

ISBN13: 978-1-032-56682-5 (hbk)
ISBN13: 978-1-032-56683-2 (pbk)
ISBN13: 978-1-003-43676-8 (ebk)

DOI: 10.4324/ 9781003436768

Typeset in Minion Pro
by codeMantra

Publisher's Note
The publisher accepts responsibility for any inconsistencies that may have arisen during the conversion of this book from journal articles to book chapters, namely the inclusion of journal terminology.

Disclaimer
Every effort has been made to contact copyright holders for their permission to reprint material in this book. The publishers would be grateful to hear from any copyright holder who is not here acknowledged and will undertake to rectify any errors or omissions in future editions of this book.

Contents

Citation Information vi
Notes on Contributors vii

Introduction 1
Paul Reilly and Virpi Salojärvi

1 Framing the Macedonian name dispute in Greece: Nationalistic journalism and the existential threat 6
 Minos-Athanasios Karyotakis

2 The "ultimate empathy machine" as technocratic solutionism? Audience reception of the distant refugee crisis through virtual reality 35
 Zhe Xu and Mengrong Zhang

3 A systemic functional linguistics approach to analyzing white supremacist and conspiratorial discourse on YouTube 58
 Olivia Inwood and Michele Zappavigna

4 Internet regulation and crisis-related resilience: From Covid-19 to existential risks 89
 Gregory Asmolov

Index 113

Citation Information

The chapters in this book were originally published in the journal *The Communication Review*, volume 25, issue 3–4 (2022). When citing this material, please use the original page numbering for each article, as follows:

Introduction
(De)constructing societal threats during times of deep mediatization
Paul Reilly and Virpi Salojärvi
The Communication Review, volume 25, issue 3–4 (2022) pp. 147–151

Chapter 1
Framing the Macedonian name dispute in Greece: Nationalistic journalism and the existential threat
Minos-Athanasios Karyotakis
The Communication Review, volume 25, issue 3–4 (2022) pp. 152–180

Chapter 2
The "ultimate empathy machine" as technocratic solutionism? Audience reception of the distant refugee crisis through virtual reality
Zhe Xu and Mengrong Zhang
The Communication Review, volume 25, issue 3–4 (2022) pp. 181–203

Chapter 3
A systemic linguistics approach to analyzing white supremacist and conspiratorial discourse on YouTube
Olivia Inwood and Michele Zappavigna
The Communication Review, volume 25, issue 3–4 (2022) pp. 204–234

Chapter 4
Internet regulation and crisis-related resilience: From Covid-19 to existential risks
Gregory Asmolov
The Communication Review, volume 25, issue 3–4 (2022) pp. 235–257

For any permission-related enquiries please visit:
http://www.tandfonline.com/page/help/permissions

Notes on Contributors

Gregory Asmolov, Department of Digital Humanities, King's College London, UK.

Olivia Inwood, School of the Arts and Media, University of New South Wales, Sydney, Australia.

Minos-Athanasios Karyotakis, School of Communication and Department of Government and International Studies, Hong Kong Baptist University, Kowloon, Hong Kong.

Paul Reilly, School of Social and Political Sciences, University of Glasgow, UK.

Virpi Salojärvi, School of Marketing and Communication, University of Vaasa, Finland; Faculty of Social Sciences, University of Helsinki, Finland.

Zhe Xu, Faculty of Arts and Humanities, University of Cologne, Germany.

Michele Zappavigna, School of the Arts and Media, University of New South Wales, Sydney, Australia.

Mengrong Zhang, Faculty of Arts and Humanities, University of Cologne, Germany.

Introduction

Paul Reilly and Virpi Salojärvi

This special issue focuses on mediatizations of societal threats in the era of hybrid media. Mediatization is a theoretical framework which has evolved somewhat in parallel with media ecologies. It was originally defined as the "growing intrusion of media logic as an institutional rule into fields where other rules of defining appropriate behavior prevailed" (Esser & Matthes, 2013, p. 177). Much of the early work in this area focused on the processes whereby modern media constrained and directly influenced the behavior of political actors (Maurer & Pfetsch, 2014; Strömbäck, 2008), as well as other institutions like the military (Maltby, 2012). However, this arguably goes much further than media-centric approaches which privilege the internationalization of media logics over other factors. Kissas (2019, p. 236) disentangles mediatization from this media centrism through the prism of "media performativity" i.e., the ways in which power is wielded within the context of mediatized politics. What is increasingly clear is that we live in deeply mediatized, datafied societies characterized by fragmented audiences that pose a challenge to the hegemony of established media and political institutions (Couldry & Hepp, 2018). While legacy media emain influential in the construction of societal threats, audiences increasingly experience these via platforms that, nominally at least, appear beyond the control of political elites.

Hoskins and O'Loughlin (2015) argue that we are currently in the third phase of mediatization. This new paradigm has seen legacy media and military institutions harness the chaotic dynamics of user-generated content in order to re-assert the agenda-setting power they exercised prior to the social media era. Yet, politicians' dependence on social media continues to create opportunities for underreported conflicts, such as the Syrian civil war, to appear on parliamentary agendas (Herrero-Jiménez, Carratalá, & Berganza, 2018). While it may be overly optimistic to suggest we are witnessing a shift in informational power from elites to non-elites, there do appear to be more fluid opportunity structures for marginalized groups to shape news agendas and be heard online (Chadwick, 2017; Creta, 2021). To this end, scholars such as Zhang (2021) have applied Actor Network Theory (ANT) to theorize the networked relationships between mainstream media, online platforms, and web users in mediatized conflicts. A similar dynamic can be observed in how elite and non-elite actors used sites like Twitter to curate information flows during crisis situations (Reilly & Vicari, 2021). People experience these events through the content shared via both legacy and digital media outlets. This raises important questions not only about their ability to shape public attitudes and behaviors, but also how they should be regulated.

This Special Issue is based on research presented in the Crisis, Security and Conflict Communication working group at the conference of International Association for Media and Communication Research (IAMCR) in 2021. It adds to this literature on mediatization by focusing specifically on how societal threats are constructed and deconstructed within deeply mediatized societies. While previous research in the field has tended to focus on how mainstream media and elite institutions have reasserted their agenda-setting power during conflict (see Hoskins & O'Loughlin, 2015 for example), we focus here on how a range of actors construct societal threats and how audiences respond to these frames. These papers bring together a range of traditional and innovative research methodologies to explore how societal threats are framed within deeply mediatized societies, ranging from content analysis of newspaper coverage of the Macedonian name dispute in Greece to investigating conspiratorial communities on YouTube using Systemic Functional Linguistics. Each one addresses how societal threats are constructed by a variety of actors, using both "old" and "new" media technologies within hybrid media ecologies.

Our first article examines how legacy media play a key role in constructing existential threats to contemporary societies. In "Framing the Macedonian Name Dispute in Greece: Nationalistic Journalism and the Existential Threat," Minos-Athanasios Karyotakis argues that media frames continue to exert great influence on public opinion in an era of deep mediatization. Drawing on a content analysis of 615 articles published in 127 news outlets, he provides evidence of how news media shaped people's perceptions of the 2018 Prespes Agreement to settle the 150-year-old Macedonian Name Dispute. Left-leaning publications heralded the agreement between Greece and the Former Yugoslav Republic of Macedonia as a key achievement of the Syriza-led government. However, the majority of Greek news outlets framed the Agreement as posing a grave threat to Greek democracy and deployed populist frames which depicted then Prime Minister Alexis Tsipras as having committed an act of "national treason." Noticeably, Karyotakis finds that the views of North Macedonians about the Agreement were conspicuously absent in coverage which sought to empower ethnic identities within Greece against this 'existential' threat to its nationhood.

The other articles in the Special Issue focus on how information and communication technologies (ICTs) are used by non-elite actors to both construct and deconstruct societal threats. "The 'ultimate empathy machine' as technocratic solutionism? Audience reception of the distant refugee crisis through Virtual Reality" examines the mediatization of the refugee crisis. Zhe Xu and Mengrong Zhang critically evaluate the techno-utopian claim that Virtual Reality can help deconstruct barriers and prejudices within contemporary societies by bringing people closer to the suffering of others. Drawing on the results of focus groups and interviews conducted in China, Germany, and the United Kingdom, they interrogate whether the United Nations (UN) VR project can transform audience attitudes toward refugee and migrant communities. They find that VR facilitates ironic consumerism rather than the emergence of cosmopolitan publics, who are empowered to take action to remedy the systemic injustices experienced by migrants and refugees. While people may in theory be closer to this distant suffering, there needs to be a greater focus on how technologies like VR are being used rather than a technological determinism which suggests that their use will create a more empathetic citizenry.

While the UN uses VR to deconstruct negative stereotypes of refugees, uncivil actors use ICTs to exclude and stigmatize those groups that they believe pose a threat to their respective societies. Online platforms in particular have emerged as key communicative spaces for White Supremacists, due in no small part to the tendency for people to experience crisis situations through User-Generated-Content (UGC). Our third paper focuses specifically on how the video-sharing platform YouTube is used to amplify and disseminate White Supremacist discourses. In "A Systemic Functional Linguistics Approach to Analysing White Supremacist and Conspiratorial Discourse on YouTube," Olivia Inwood and Michele Zappavigna examine the mediatization of these discourses through the case study of the Notre Dame Fire in April 2019. The first study of its kind to use Systemic Functional Linguistics (SFL) to investigate conspiratorial discourses online, their results show that white supremacists used affiliation strategies to convince audiences that Muslims had deliberately started the fire. While Karyotakis posits that legacy media continues to play a key role in constructing societal threats experienced by citizens, platform affordances enable these conspiratorial communities to appeal to the social bonds and values of their audiences in order to "other" Muslims. Conceivably the amplification and circulation of these conspiracy theories could have negative implications for societal resilience to future crisis situations. Inwood and Zappavigna demonstrate how SFL can provide invaluable insight into the mediatization of such incidents.

Societal resilience toward crises and disasters also concerns the author of our last paper. Mediatization has clearly transformed the nature of crisis situations due to the degree to which citizens' lives have become entangled with digital media infrastructures. Online platforms empower citizens through the creation of early warning systems and their use to mobilize resources as part of disaster response initiatives (Reilly & Atanasova, 2016). In "Internet Regulation and Crisis-Related Resilience: From Covid-19 to Existential Risks," Gregory Asmolov asks whether internet regulation might have a detrimental impact on the generative capacity of online platforms during such incidents. Drawing on evidence gathered from 15 COVID-19-related initiatives in Russia, Asmolov argues that the internet regulation introduced in order to counteract mis- and disinformation about the pandemic may counterintuitively diminish the ability of policymakers to leverage the affordances of online platforms during future crises. Asmolov proposes a methodological framework, which focuses on objects, subjects, and platforms as mediating tools, to assess the impact of internet regulation on the capacity of online platforms to facilitate citizen-led initiatives in response to future crises.

Deep mediatization presents both challenges and opportunities for policymakers responding to crises and threats. Both civil and uncivil actors leverage the affordances of ICTs in order to appeal to the values of audiences, who increasingly experience these events through these media technologies. While the extent to which these frames change the attitudes and behaviors of citizens merits further investigation, the papers in this Special Issue undoubtedly enrich our understanding of how societal threats are both constructed and deconstructed within deeply mediatized societies

Disclosure statement

No potential conflict of interest was reported by the authors.

ORCID

Virpi Salojärvi http://orcid.org/0000-0001-9596-8804

References

Chadwick, A. (2017). *The hybrid media system: Politics and power* (2nd ed.). Oxford: Oxford University Press.
Couldry, N., & Hepp, A. (2018). The continuing lure of the mediated centre in times of deep mediatization: Media events and its enduring legacy. *Media, Culture & Society*, *40*(1), 114–117. doi:10.1177/0163443717726
Creta, S. (2021). I hope, one day, I will have the right to speak. *Media, War & Conflict*, *14*(3), 366–382. doi:10.1177/1750635221989566
Esser, F., & Matthes, J. (2013). Mediatization effects on political news, political actors, political decisions, and political audiences. In H. Kriesi, S. Lavanex, F. Esser, & J. Matthes & others

(Eds.), *Democracy in the age of globalization and mediatization* (pp. 177–201). London: Palgrave Macmillan.

Herrero-Jiménez, B., Carratalá, A., & Berganza, R. (2018). Violent conflicts and the new mediatization: The impact of social media on the European Parliamentary agenda regarding the Syrian War. *Communication & Society*, *31*(3), 141–157. doi:10.15581/003.31.3.141-155

Hoskins, A., & O'Loughlin, B. (2015). Arrested war: The third phase of mediatization. *Information, Communication & Society*, *18*(11), 1320–1338. doi:10.1080/1369118X.2015.1068350

Kissas, A. (2019). Three theses on the mediatization of politics: Evolutionist, intended, or imagined transformation? *The Communication Review*, *22*(3), 222–242. doi:10.1080/10714421.2019.1647726

Maltby, S. (2012). The mediatization of the military. *Media, War & Conflict*, *5*(3), 255–268. doi:10.1177/1750635212447908

Maurer, P., & Pfetsch, B. (2014). News coverage of politics and conflict levels. *Journalism Studies*, *153*, 339–355. doi:10.1080/1461670X.2014.889477

Reilly, P. J., & Atanasova, D. (2016). A report on the media and information flows during crisis situations, EU FP7 cascEff project deliverable 3.4, European Commission FP7.

Reilly, P. J., & Vicari, S. (2021). Organisational hashtags during times of crisis: Analysing the broadcasting and gatekeeping dynamics of #PorteOuverte during the November 2015 Paris Terror Attacks. *Social Media + Society*, January 2021. doi:10.1177/2056305121995788

Strömbäck, J. (2008). Four phases of mediatization: An analysis of the mediatization of politics. *The International Journal of Press/Politics*, *13*(3), 228–246. doi:10.1177/1940161208319097

Zhang, S. I. (2021). Mediatization of conflict in the social media era: A case study of the Sino-Indian border crisis in 2017. *Journalism*, *22*(10), 2618–2636. doi:10.1177/1464884919987032

Framing the Macedonian name dispute in Greece: Nationalistic journalism and the existential threat

Minos-Athanasios Karyotakis

ABSTRACT

In the Macedonian Name Dispute (MND), the Greek media promoted the country's main nationalistic narrative that treats the compromise between Greece and its neighboring country (now-named North Macedonia) as a national crisis that could even lead to an existential threat to Greece and its people. To investigate the recent events related to the MND, this study examined 615 news articles throughout 2018 and 2019 to identify how the news media framed the events associated with the MND and the Prespes Agreement. The results revealed that most news stories framed the MND incidents as a political or mobilization tool of the public and an existential threat to Greece. Furthermore, the news coverage showed that several news stories employed the patriotic and nationalistic frame to support or undermine the country's then-government. These findings offer insights into the use of territorial name disputes as a communication tool, how news articles and journalism promote the idea of an existential threat connected to the MND, and the alarming non-critical news coverage that could lead to a further democratic backsliding of Greece.

Introduction

The Macedonian Name Dispute (MND) is considered one of the oldest name disputes in the world as it is connected with the Macedonian Question, the collapse of Yugoslavia, and the emergence of the nation-state called at this moment Republic of North Macedonia. The dispute is around 150 years old, and in the last 30 years, it was developed between Greece and North Macedonia. The main problem was that Greece did not want to give its neighboring country the name Macedonia, as it is an essential part of the Greek cultural heritage. By agreeing to name Greece's neighboring country Macedonia, the Greeks would have lost essential identity elements. For instance, the heritage of Alexander the Great would not be anymore a monopoly of Greece. Moreover, in the country's national narrative, there could even be territorial losses despite the plethora of agreements securing the borders of both states (Heraclides, 2019).

The MND seemed to be solved at the beginning of 2019 with the ratification of the "Prespes Agreement" that gave Greece's neighboring country the name Macedonia. This accord was perceived as national treason by several prominent news outlets and provoked many prominent demonstrations. Moreover, the government that realized the accord was led by the radical left party called Syriza (2015–2019). Syriza became the main rival of New Democracy's (ND) right-wing party taking the position of PASOK (Panhellenic Socialist Movement) in 2012 as Greece's second most popular party after the unprecedented financial crisis that shook the country and its political system in 2008. The Greeks believed that the "Prespes Agreement" was the realization of the existential threat (loss of Macedonia's monopoly) that they were so afraid of. Subsequently, they empowered ND in the local, European, and national elections in 2019. ND won all the elections, and despite its claims for altering the "treacherous Prespes Agreement," nothing changed. On the contrary ND started promoting the "Prespes Agreement" and the stronger ties with North Macedonia (Kitsantonis, 2018; Antonopoulos, 2020b; Amna.gr, 2019; Ekathimerini.com, 2019; Hall & Hope, 2019).

After the win of the national elections, the new government of ND, with the help of several news outlets, started to hide the truth, as Kyriakos Mitsotakis and ND were eventually in favor of the agreement that gave the neighboring country a part of Greece's identity (Macedonian, name, language, and ethnicity). Furthermore, there seemed to be several cases of censoring press releases, altering facts, and forgetting to report issues related to the MND (Kanellopoulos, 2020; Left.gr, 2019; Michalopoulos, 2019, 2020). As a result, it can be argued that it was not an accident that throughout 2018 and 2019, several influential news outlets were promoting statements like those mentioned above.

The dissemination of the non-solution for the MND in order to support the downfall of the then-government is linked with the electoral and mobilization power associated with the MND. From the 1990s until the national elections of 2019, almost all of the most prominent politicians and parties have exploited it to gain significant electoral power. Furthermore, the MND has provoked some of the most massive demonstrations in the history of the country, including probably the largest one on 14th February 1992, in which around a million Greeks gathered in Thessaloniki to protest in favor of the Greekness of Macedonia. In addition, the protesters were arguing that the people of North Macedonia were trying to steal parts of the Greek identity (Heraclides, 2019).

In the Greek state's main nationalistic narrative, Macedonia can only be Greek, and, thus, the majority of the news media have not actually challenged this narrative (Demertzis, Papathanassopoulos, & Armenakis, 1999; Ellinas, 2010). After all, the Greek news media are known for low professionalism and are not keen on preserving their watchdog role. In addition, the Greek media system is characterized by a constant interplay between the media and the politicians based on clientelism (Hallin & Mancini, 2004; Papathanassopoulos, 2017).

Clientelism is a phenomenon that has become more prominent around the world, as it can play a decisive role in the democratic backslide and the form of new regimes, such as despotisms (Chowdhury & Keane, 2021; Keane, 2020). Adding to this, Greece is considered one of the most prominent and successful examples of nationalism in creating an independent nation-state worldwide (Smith, 2010). Nationalism is used as a media and populistic tool for mobilizing the public through different tactics, such as spreading hate and creating existential threats (securitized issues) (Karyotakis, 2021a).

However, there is no research focusing on the news coverage of the recent events of the MND that led to the so-called "Prespes Agreement" that was received as a solution to this everlasting dispute by many prominent global actors such as Germany, the United States of America (USA), United Kingdom (UK), to name a few (Vankovska, 2020). MND has been used for many years as a tool for electoral power (Ellinas, 2010). As a result, the current study investigates how news articles and journalism promote the idea of an existential threat connected to the MND and a dominant narrative that is strongly associated with Greek nationalism.

It is known that the news media can empower a group's ethnic identity through the dissemination of nationalistic news stories promoting the idea of a unique nation that is different from any other (Erjavec & Volčič, 2007). Nevertheless, the solution to the MND with the "Prespes Agreement" seemed to empower Greece's position in the Balkans. For example, Greece started policing the airspace of North Macedonia (Kampouris, 2019).

Therefore, the current study explores the news media's frames (615 news articles from 127 news outlets) of the recent events associated with the MND through a qualitative interpretative method of framing analysis as such an approach "examines the keywords, metaphors, narratives, and so on, in context of the text as a whole" (Connolly-Ahern & Broadway, 2008, p. 369). In particular, the manuscript focuses on the Securitization Theory (existential threat), nationalism, and nationalistic journalism, to explain the dominant frames and topics of three different periods (14–28 January 2018, 19 May-3 June 2019, and 30 June-14 July 2019).

the importance of the MND

The MND belongs to the territorial disputes that are developed between state-actors. Because territories are essential parts of the nation-states' dominant nationalistic narratives, the countries usually go against each other. As a result, they are considered a powerful resource for the mobilization of people. Those disputes are usually preserved in the people's collective memory to remind them of how vicious the neighboring countries are. It is not a surprise that their use can provoke extreme actions, such as a war between the conflicting sides. Nevertheless, these disputes are used as proxies for realizing other more essential goals. The territorial claims are not the main reason for waging war or provoking public rage (Chubin & Tripp, 1993; Dunbar, 2000; Hayton, 2017).

One such recent example can be the war between Armenia and Azerbaijan in the Nagorno-Karabakh region. Both countries wanted to secure the disputed area for reasons that are not related so much to their nationalistic narratives. Therefore, that is one reason why there is substantial interference by Iran, Russia, and Turkey in that particular conflict (Cornell, 1998; Waal, 2010). Turkey's reasons for helping Azerbaijan are not related to the emotional arguments of its President, Recep Tayyip Erdoğan, who argued that Turkey and Azerbaijan are "two states, one nation" (Trtworld.com, 2020). Turkey has strong financial interests in Azerbaijan concerning the energy industry. The Nagorno-Karabakh conflict can disrupt the gas and oil exports of the region. Azerbaijan plays a vital role in the energy industry for Europe and Central Asia (Cfr.org, 2020; Winrow, 2009).

Despite the common use of the name "Nagorno-Karabakh," Armenia seems to prefer to refer to the region as "Artsakh" in order to maintain the idea that the region belongs to Armenia instead of Azerbaijan. "Artsakh" was a region of the ancient Kingdom of Armenia thousands of years ago. On the other hand, the Azerbaijani side and its news outlets tend not to refer to the disputed territory as "Artsakh" to empower the Armenian claims (Kolstø & Blakkisrud, 2012; Ghazanchyan, 2020; Antonopoulos, 2020a; Dabaghyan, 2011).

In Nagorno-Karabakh, there are actual territorial claims, and one of the communication techniques for preserving these nationalistic narratives and arguments is the use of a different name. However, what happens if there are different names in a territorial claim with no actual territorial claims?

The MND, like other important disputes of the globe, such as The Persian Gulf/The Arabian Gulf, has no actual territorial claims, as there are international treaties that secure the warring sides' borders. Nevertheless, the territorial dispute remains prominent throughout the years, leading to a contentious communication process that involves extreme accusations against the involved sides and an influential war of words in the public discourse. Each side uses a different name to overwrite the other conflicting narrative and maintain its own as the legitimate one (Isidoros, 2017; Kostopoulos & Psarras, 2018). Despite the prominence of this communication phenomenon and its power, the game of names in territorial disputes has not been researched from a communication and journalism perspective.

Consequently, the current study examines the news coverage frames throughout the years 2018 & 2019, in which the MND dominated the public and media discourse in Greece. Thus, it will also provide insights into the game of names in territorial disputes, the ways journalism promotes the idea of an existential threat, and dominant narratives that empower nationalism.

MND, like other territorial name disputes, has been used for many years successfully in empowering those politicians and news outlets that repeat the main nationalistic narrative of the country that forbids the reference to Greece's neighboring country as "Macedonia." The research of the news outlets' frames throughout that critical period is believed to provide insights into the news outlets' tactics in their coverage and shed light on the under-researched topic of the game of names in territorial disputes.

Nationalism, the existential threat, and nationalistic journalism

Nationalism has not a standard definition, but there is a consensus that it is a movement that promotes and supports the ideas expressed by a dominant community for a common ideological construction that includes a shared identity and the potential of creating a nation that aims in preserving its governance and sovereignty. That shared constructed identity is preserved and empowered by the unity and the enlargement of this group based on the shared common characteristics (Crawford, 2012; Smith, 2010).

For keeping alive this shared ideological construction called nation, the community has to preserve the main narrative that will be passed down from one generation to the other. That procedure is mostly happening with cultural products (e.g., media) and their dissemination through each country's nationalistic education, which involves selecting specific narratives and representations of a historical truth that highlights the group's importance against the others. These historical facts, along with national legends and myths, tend to strengthen and maintain unchallenged this large community that forms a nation (Baycroft, 2005).

Therefore, according to Anderson (2016), these constructed entities called nations were imagined communities, as they were created through imagined elements, including the selection of a convenient past for each nation. Language also was one of those elements that contributed to constructing the common identity that shaped a nation-state. That is why it is essential for the Greeks that their national ideology the nonrecognition of the Macedonian language. By recognizing the Macedonian language, Greece would have to accept that there is a clear distinction between the Greeks and the Macedonians. Besides, it has to be considered that Greece was one of the most prominent examples worldwide that exploited the element of language for revolting against the Ottoman Empire, claiming their territorial sovereignty and creating eventually the nation-state called Greece. Furthermore, the idea of the barbarians occupying the territory of ancient Greece who had forgotten their true identity was shared amongst prominent intellectuals in Europe. Subsequently, the barbarians had to regain their true self through the common Greek values and become once again the proper ancestors of the ancient Greeks (Anderson, 2016).

For the construction of a nation-state, there is also a need to create and disseminate an existential threat. The manufacture of an existential threat (or security threat) through a communication process can be explained by the Securitization Theory (ST), which comes from the field of International Relations (IR). In the beginning, ST was supposed to develop an improved theoretical framework and understanding for revealing the different dimensions of war, including the construction of an existential threat. Therefore, it is believed that such a securitization process can provoke powerful emotions and even result in a consensus amongst the government or state officials and the public (Balzacq, 2005; Buzan, Wæver, & Wilde, 1998). The construction of an existential threat (or security threat) goes beyond the security studies tradition. Buzan, Waever, and de Wilde created securitization Theory in their book Security: A new framework for analysis (Buzan et al., 1998). The main difference between this new approach and the tradition of IR is that Buzan and his colleagues pointed out that a security process can include various incidents and concepts, such as the identity and the Environment, raising, in the meantime, questions about the moral aspects of creating such a threat (see Floyd, 2019; Floyd & Croft, 2019).

Waever was the one that presented first his ideas about this new approach in security studies by arguing that there must be a more in-depth focus on the existed societal discourse. For Waever (Lipschutz, 1995), there was already a common understanding amongst people about a security issue (or threat) in society, as society is thought to be a more harmonious and pleasant place if there is more security. Therefore, Buzan et al. (1998) argued that researchers must focus even on nonmilitary issues, as even unimportant topics can become actual existential threats in the mind of the people. However, in order to do so, there must be a successful securitization process:

> A successful securitization thus has three components (or steps): existential threats, emergency actions, and effects on interunit relations by breaking free of rules. The distinguishing feature of securitization is a specific rhetorical structure (survival, priority of action 'because if the problem is not handled now it will be too late, and we will not exist to remedy our failure') (Buzan et al., 1998, p. 26).

In addition, securitization studies have pointed out that every aspect of society and every incident can become a security (or existential) threat and evoke fear throughout a process that involves communication. For example, McInnes and Rushton (2013) have proved that even health issues, such as HIV/AIDS, can be successfully securitized. Another example is the refugee crisis (Stivas, 2021), or Covid-19 with the securitization processes worldwide regarding this issue, with some scholars talking even for hyper-securitization (Stivas & Smith,

2020). The creation of fear through an existential threat in securitization studies can be explained with a widely accepted theoretical framework, which shows that every aspect of society can become an issue that evokes fear in citizens.

On the other hand, the existential threat and the emotion of fear of ethnic nationalism come from the idea of belonging and that people are born with unique characteristics that distinguish their group from the others. The core element of the sentiment of nationalism is the individual and the group that he/she belongs to. The group and the individual are distinct from the others, and it must preserve and protect these differences; otherwise, there is a creation of fear of losing its unique characteristics (Baycroft, 2005; Handman, 1921). In particular:

> The ordinary emotions and instincts become attached to them, mildly or intensely, according as these experiences are deep and tumultuous or merely superficial and passing. Under proper conditions, this system so organized may show itself in behavior as an agitated and agitating concern with the life and honor of the group (Handman, 1921, p. 104).

Adding to Handman's thoughts, "the nationalist believes that not only the others are hell, but everything which is not his (Serbian, Croatian, French...) is alien to him" (Kis, 1996, p. 14). However, for promoting these ideas throughout society, there must be several news outlets that practice nationalistic journalism. According to Ginosar (2015, p. 292) "nationalistic journalism, on the other hand, is journalism that echoes what authorities want to say or what citizens want to hear." Several post-colonial societies, for example, Ireland and Greece, are practicing often nationalistic journalism when national interests are at stake (Demertzis et al., 1999; Foley, 2004; Hallin & Mancini, 2004).

This particular kind of journalism is based on nationalistic ideology, as it uses several of its elements. For example, glorifying the country's history and past or using symbolic narratives for justifying claims about territories that are lost and must be regained. Furthermore, nationalistic journalism follows the authorities' requests and supports the dominant narratives as they are dictated by the country's nationalistic truth (Erjavec & Volčič, 2007). Besides, it "establishes loyalty toward the state power and nationalistic elites, recreates the dichotomy of an 'us-versus-them,' 'my-country-right-or-wrong' version of reporting, and forges a sense of national pride and patriotism" (Erjavec & Volčič, 2007, p. 81).

The main problem with nationalistic journalism is that it goes against one of the main values of western journalism, which is to maintain a critical opinion about the governments and the state, empowering, in the meantime, the citizens. The journalists' voice must not be the same as the governmental one (Elliott, 2004; George, 2018).

With the continuous repeating of the same nationalistic narrative, the idea of an existential threat regarding national issues can be reactivated to gain the public's support. Due to that dominant narrative, including the element of an existential threat, the public will think that demonstrating against a compromise or a possible agreement, serves its essential role of protecting the nation and protecting the "in-group" from the "out-group." A similar case can be made for the journalists and the news outlets that choose this coverage. In their mind, they are probably fulfilling their role of helping the people and the nation-state (Neiger & Rimmer-Tsory, 2012).

This recycled nationalistic narrative can also preserve the hostility toward these out-groups and mix the past with additional elements from future events to highlight why the focus on this conflict is significant and must be covered. Thus, there can be a disproportionate coverage of nationalistic issues, which under different circumstances, would not be so extensively covered (Zelizer, 2017).

Methods and data

The news stories analyzed in the current research were collected during three periods (Table 1). For studying the frames of the news coverage, the current research paper uses a qualitative interpretative method of framing analysis for presenting and also analyzing the dominant frames of the news coverage, as in the case of the MND, it seems that the coverage of news media has played a crucial role in provoking people to express nationalistic ideas and to demonstrate against a possible solution between Greece and its neighboring country.

Framing analysis is considered a popular method for analyzing how the news media influence collective thought and provoked mobilization. For example, Olesen (2015) explained in detail through the use of framing based on Gamson's ideas that the media globally can diffuse collective meanings and values shared by certain groups. The result is to demonstrate in favor of protecting these values and meanings. He also pointed out that these shared symbols are produced through politics, creating a socio-political consciousness worldwide. As a result, Olesen's idea might be relative to the study of territorial name disputes, such as the MND. The reason is that all these

Table 1. The characteristics of the study's sample.

Study's Timeframe	No. of News Stories	Keyword (In Greek)
14–28 January 2018	178	Macedonian Issue (Μακεδονικό/Makedoniko)
14–28 January 2018	173	Skopjan issue (Σκοπιανό/Skopiano)
19 May-3 June 2019	137	Prespes Agreement (Συμφωνία Πρεσπών/Symfonia Prespon)
30 June-14 July 2019	127	Prespes Agreement (Συμφωνία Πρεσπών/Symfonia Prespon)

disputes seem to share common characteristics despite occurring in other parts of the world. Furthermore, the warring sides in territorial disputes justify their claims and actions by promoting morality as another aspect of claiming what is rightful (Yorgason, 2017).

Framing is a core idea for helping individuals set up a storyline for interpreting all the related events of this storyline. In other words, the frame is supposed to be the essence of the topic (Cacciatore et al., 2016). However, Robert Entman was the scholar that made the Framing theory popular amongst researchers in the communication field. For him (Entman, 1993, p. 52), "to frame is to select some aspects of a perceived reality and make them more salient in a communicating text, in such a way as to promote a particular problem definition, causal interpretation, moral evaluation, and/or treatment recommendation for the item described."

Gamson (1990) was the scholar that explained the importance of the role of mass media organizations during events of collective actions. His framework points out that the collective actions agents require the media to help them distribute their messages. On the other hand, news organizations need collective actors to attract the audience's interest and increase their profits. In other words, Gamson and his colleagues were the first scholars that focused on interpreting the connection between collective and media actors. Building on Goffman's (1974) arguments about framing analysis, they formed an approach that is based on the tradition of sociology (Cacciatore et al., 2016).

A frame is a core idea that creates a specific narrative and, therefore, specific meanings. Moreover, frames are components of the public discourse, a more extensive "package" that includes signifiers and policies from which "symbolic devices" are generated. Journalists are crucial in that process (Gamson & Modigliani, 1989). The "symbolic devices" that construct the frames are the following ones: (a) catchphrases, (b) depictions, (c) exemplars, and (d) visual images (Pan & Kosicki, 1993).

The "symbolic devices" in the exemplars are highlighted in bold. As the study included 127 news outlets (for the detailed list of the study's news outlets, see table A1 in the appendix), there cannot be a detailed presentation of each news story. Thus, the most suitable examples (exemplars) were chosen to highlight the main dominant frames that were identified through the reading of all the full articles of the study (Table 2).

The qualitative framing analysis was used to focus on the socio-political and cultural meanings that deal with complexity (Connolly-Ahern & Broadway, 2008; Gitlin, 2003). More specifically, qualitative framing analysis "examines the keywords, metaphors, narratives, and so on, in context of the text as a whole" (Connolly-Ahern & Broadway, 2008, p. 369). Also, it "identifies what was left out of the frame as well as what was included" (Connolly-Ahern & Broadway, 2008, p. 369).

Table 2. The dominant frames of the study.

Dominant Frames	Description
The Events as Political & Mobilization Tools for Electoral Power	The events were presented as incidents that are used to mobilize the public for electoral power, as political events orchestrated by political groups and parties to win the public and realize political ambitions.
Existential Threat: Securing or Losing Greece's legacy and identity	These stories presented the Prespes Agreement as an existential threat for Greece, as the country was losing the monopoly of the name Macedonia and, thus, a part of its identity.
Greece's Superiority to North Macedonia (Nationalistic Frame) versus Securing Greece's Influence in the Balkan Region (Patriotic Frame)	The nationalistic frame refers to Greece's nationalistic narrative, promoting the uniqueness and superiority of Greece over North Macedonia. The patriotic frame goes against the nationalistic frame, arguing that the Prespes Agreement is an act of patriotism.
Prespes Agreement as Peace & International Affair	Prespes Agreement is presented as an accord that promotes peace and international relations.

Subsequently, the current study examines the specific dominant narratives-frames promoted by the Greek news outlets during the periods mentioned earlier.

The three different periods of the frame study

The search of news articles for the study was performed through Google Search Engine and included every possible news story and news outlet in Greece based on Google Search, aiming to provide a big picture of the media content of that period.

RQ: What are the dominant frames of the news coverage of the Prespes Agreement in the Greek media?

The first period covered was from 14 to 28 January 2018. At the end of January, the public discussion started concerning a possible solution to the MND. The coverage period straddled the date of probably the most important MND demonstration in Greece for the recent MND events, on 21 January 2018 at Thessaloniki (Dw.com, 2018).

Thessaloniki is considered the capital of the so-called Land of Macedonia (the region that includes the Macedonian territories that expand into nations such as Greece, North Macedonia, and Bulgaria). Consequently, Thessaloniki had always been an important symbolic power for the MND (Mazower, 2006). Moreover, it was the city that has experienced probably the most massive demonstration in Greece's history. That demonstration was for the MND in 1992, in which around a million people flooded the city to express their anger against a solution with North Macedonia (Chrysopoulos, 2018).

The collection of the news stories was conducted by using the keywords "Macedonian Issue" (Μακεδονικό/Makedoniko) and "Skopjan issue"

(Σκοπιανό/Skopiano) in Greek. The search with the keyword "Macedonian Issue" (Μακεδονικό/Makedoniko) provided 178 news stories, and the other one with the keyword "Skopjan issue" (Σκοπιανό/Skopiano) gave 173 news stories (208 was the initial number of the search, but it ended up as 173 after removing the duplicate news stories with the "Macedonian Issue" (Μακεδονικό/Makedoniko).

The keyword ("Skopjan issue") was used in the Greek media and public discourse as it is the preferred term for referring to the MND. For some Macedonians, the term "Skopjan" is racist, as it is continuously used by the Greeks to undermine the neighboring country and its claims. It is also a term that promotes the idea of a Greek cultural and economic superiority over North Macedonia (Macedonianhr.org.au, n.d.).

The second period studied was from the 19th of May to the 3rd of June 2019. The collection of the news stories was performed by using the keyword "Prespes Agreement (Συμφωνία Πρεσπών/Symfonia Prespon) in Greek. It provided 137 news stories.

That timeframe was selected to explore the frames during the coverage of the local and European elections on the 26th of May 2019. In the Greek electoral system, the two most prominent candidates for becoming mayors in each city that they could not collect more than 50% percent of the votes had to compete in a run-off on the 2nd of June 2019. The local and European elections were significant as the incumbent Syriza suffered a heavy defeat by ND. That electoral defeat led Syriza's leader and Greece's then-Prime Minister to announce earlier the national elections that instead of happening at the end of 2019, were organized on the 7th of July 2019 (Euractiv.com, 2019a; Thenationalnews.com, 2019).

The third and last search of the study covered the period of 30 June until 14 July 2019. The collection of the news stories was performed by using the keyword "Prespes Agreement (Συμφωνία Πρεσπών/Symfonia Prespon) in Greek. It provided 127 news stories. That timeframe was chosen to investigate the national elections (7 July 2019) that led to the defeat of Syriza that realized the "Prespes Agreement," the change of the Greek government with the win of ND, and the election of Kyriakos Mitsotakis as the new Prime Minister.

Results

The events as political & mobilization tools for electoral power

The use of the MND as a political and mobilization tool was the most common frame of the examined news articles (Figure 1). The warring sides, mostly the two main political parties of Greece (ND & Syriza), were accusing each other

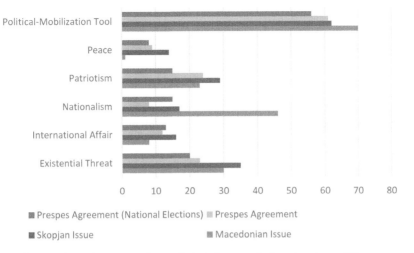

Figure 1. The number of news stories and their frames during the three different examined periods.

of exploiting the MND to gain electoral power. For Syriza, the use of the MND seemed to be strongly associated with the effort of ND to attract the interest of the extreme right-wing individuals and to obtain their votes (Exemplar 1).

Exemplar 1: Opinion column

The **extreme right turn of Mr. Mitsotakis**, due to the fear of founding a party "on the right" of ND after the rally in Thessaloniki, has **opened Aeolus' bag inside the ND**. The leader of the official opposition's position **in favor of the rallies** and his assessment that the solution for the "Macedonian issue" "**should be sought in another situation**" brought to the **surface the dichotomy inside the ND** (Avgi.gr, 2018).

On the other hand, in the beginning, ND seemed not to take a clear stance against solving the dispute. However, after the massive demonstration in Thessaloniki, many of its members started to be more critical of a possible solution. In addition, some members that were not so extreme regarding their stance against North Macedonia were removed from their positions to give space to those politicians that wanted to support the "Greekness of Macedonia" and the idea that Greece cannot give the name Macedonia to its neighboring country. Such a prominent example was the case of Vasiliki Eftaxa, the Chairman of the Governing Committee of ND in Thessaloniki, who "had advised the local executives to keep their distance from initiatives such as rallies or the signing of announcements/texts for the Skopjan issue" (Enikonomia.gr, 2018).

Despite the initial response of ND, which was not clear enough if the party was against a possible solution to the name dispute, the other two examined periods for this study showed that the tactic of supporting the extreme opinion concerning the Greekness of Macedonia became more powerful and more evident. Several of the most influential ND politicians were accusing Syriza of trying to solve the dispute to win the support of those who were more progressive and with left-wing ideological backgrounds, instead of listening to the people's voice that demanded not to realize such an Agreement (Exemplar 2).

Exemplar 2: Interview with an ND politician

It is obvious that **people feel betrayed. The vast majority did not agree to the signing of the Agreement but this was ignored by the government**. The **Prespes Agreement** did not solve the old problem but **added new ones to the region** (Petropoulou, 2019).

Lastly, the examined news articles revealed a disproportionate coverage in favor of the voices against a solution to the dispute (Figure 2). In particular, during the incidents related to Thessaloniki's demonstration, many articles were promoting radical or far-right-wing ideas from the rallies' organizers who were branded as neo-Macedonian Fighters (Makedonomachoi) from the Macedonian Struggle (Fotopoulos, 2019; Gounaris, 2007). However, the promotion of their initiatives was declined after the rumors of creating a new right-wing party that would express the viewpoints of all those in favor of Macedonia's Greekness.

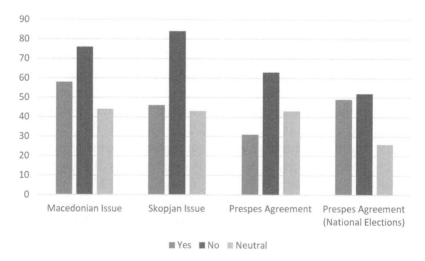

Figure 2. The number of news stories favoring (Yes) or opposing (No) a possible solution to the MND (e.g., Prespes Agreement), and the neutral ones (Neutral) during the three examined periods of the study.

Existential threat: securing or losing Greece's legacy and identity

The second most common frame throughout the examined period is the idea of an existential threat promoted by different influential actors who hold power in Greek society. The two main narratives connected with the idea of an existential threat were arguing that in the case that there is no solution, then the results will be dreadful for Greece, as it is probably the last chance for the country for agreeing with North Macedonia and securing its true legacy that is exploited by the neighboring state. The politicians that were in favor of the "Prespes Agreement" mainly promoted that narrative (Exemplar 3).

Exemplar 3: Senior diplomat quoted in a news story

If FYROM joins NATO **without the constitutional ratification of the new name** and the **deletion of the redemptive articles in the Constitution, Greece will have no more leverage, and any agreements will probably remain a blank slate** (Enikonomia.gr, 2018b).

The other narrative claimed that with the agreement, Greece is losing parts of its legacy and identity, and, thus, it is of the greatest importance of securing the non-ratification of the accord and the fall of the government that is betraying the people's will. Furthermore, the existential threat frame in both cases seemed to preserve an idea of territorial losses against Greece in the future. If there was no Agreement, Turkey would have developed closer connections with North Macedonia to undermine Greece's influential position in the Balkans (Exemplar 4).

Exemplar 4: Interview with an ND politician

The **Prespes Agreement is nationally damaging**. This is already visible to everyone, as **problems and threats arise everywhere**, with the crowning of the issues of the so-called "Macedonian" identity that the government has given to its northern neighbors ... **nothing is over** (Euractiv.gr, 2019b).

The frame of the existential threat and its association with the name dispute resolution was detected almost exclusively in articles against Syriza and the parties that seemed willing to support a solution. Those news articles were based mostly on statements from ND's politicians. In addition, many news outlets were disseminating the idea of an existential threat by interviewing celebrities favoring the Greekness of Macedonia. Therefore, Syriza seemed not to promote the idea of the existential threat against Greece firmly if there was non-ratification of the "Prespes Agreement." After the massive demonstrations and the loss of the local and EU elections by the ND, the then-government tried to highlight patriotism, which is with the nationalistic frame of the other most common frames identified in the current research.

Greece's superiority to North Macedonia (Nationalistic frame) versus securing Greece's influence in the Balkan region (Patriotic frame)

During the coverage of the events related to Thessaloniki's demonstration, the use of the nationalistic frame was more prominent. The new media were underling the Greek national narrative's core ideas about Macedonia and that it can only be Greek, as it is linked with the essential parts of the Greek identity. Those news stories' characteristic was that they supported an idea of Greece's superiority over North Macedonia. As a powerful country with a significant cultural heritage and legacy, Greece should not accept that a little country like North Macedonia is trying to steal its history and traditions. Consequently, there should be no negotiations and discussions with the neighboring country (Exemplar 5).

Exemplar 5: Interview with an ND politician

First of all, the **Macedonians are never going to call the Slavs "Macedonians." For us, Macedonia is an exclusive Greek heritage, part of our history, part of our soul**. And this heritage is not fragmented. **History is not rewritten, and our soul is not sold**. We will work, therefore, to develop and highlight everywhere in the world, **the eternal Macedonia. And it is good for our neighbors to remember that their journey to Europe passes through Athens** (Tovima.gr, 2019).

Contrary to the nationalistic frame, the then-government tried to frame its actions through its news media and members' statements for realizing the "Prespes Agreement" as a patriotic act. Despite the harsh arguments of the opposition parties, that particular act of patriotism was securing Greece's interests and influence in the Balkan region. Moreover, it was bringing back Macedonia to Greece, as the signed accord was clarifying that the heritage linked with the ancient kingdom of Macedonia and its leading figures, such as Alexander the Great and his father, are associated with Greece. Besides, it was clarified that the Macedonian language is indeed a language with Slavic origins. As a result, there can be no connection between the language and ancient Greece or Macedonia's ancient kingdom. Consequently, such an important agreement that secures and empowers Greece can only be perceived as a patriotic act, especially if it is considered that Syriza was the only party that supported and ratified the agreement from the beginning despite the apparent loss of electoral power (Exemplar 6).

Exemplar 6: Interview with a Syriza politician

The populism that prevailed in the media and the opposition parties is unbelievable. Monstrous things have been said that have nothing to do with the truth. **If one reads the Prespes Agreement, Greece has taken back its own history.** Whereas before, **the people of Skopje appropriated Greek history. Nowadays, this is not happening. Today the neighboring state is called North Macedonia for everyone, not "Macedonia"** (Arcadiaportal.gr, 2019).

Prespes agreement as peace & international affair

The least two common frames promoted by the news media were the peace and international affair frame. The first one was based mostly on statements by those politicians and parties that supported solving the MND. As a result, the "Prespes Agreement" was an essential step for the further peaceful development amongst the Balkan countries. In addition, the news stories based on the peaceful resolution of the dispute were also disseminating the importance of the accord for the European Union's future. Therefore, it was not a surprise that all the stories using this frame favored the "Prespes Agreement" (Exemplar 7).

Exemplar 7: Syriza's politician quoted in a news story

For the **Prespes Agreement**, he [Euclid Tsakalotos] described it as a **"landmark in Greek society and Greek politics,"** not only as he said, "because the Left managed to provide **a solution to a problem that had been pending for 23 years** but because it showed that it is part of the solution and not the problem. **Peace and development in the Balkans is a strategic choice**" (Naftemporiki.gr, 2019).

The news outlets that framed their articles as an international affair were mostly focused on prominent politicians who were usually not Greeks. The statements and the news articles' framing were almost exclusively positive for the then-government and its efforts to solve the name dispute. However, a few negative ones argued that the solution is being imposed by other most powerful countries to Greece, such as Germany and the USA, to fulfill their greater plans for gaining more power in the region. Greece had to follow their wills and advice, as the "Prespes Agreement" was not a bilateral issue but a dispute that impacted an international level. According to this narrative, the then-government through the "Prespes Agreement" would get more help from those major countries (Exemplar 8).

Exemplar 8: News story

Alexis Tsipras' interview with the Financial Times had **a cynical confession regarding the opening of the case of the name of Skopje** that led to the Prespes Agreement and the name of North Macedonia ... **He describes a meeting they had in Berlin and a discussion about the financial crisis, the debt, the surpluses, and the memoranda** (Parapolitika.gr, 2019).

Despite that the news organizations framed the events related to the MND and the Prespes Agreement as an international affair that promotes peace or an accord forced by the more powerful nations, what is missing is the frames and the viewpoints from the part of North Macedonia. The Greek news outlets in the examined timeframes seem not to pay at all efforts to present the other side's frames of the name dispute.

Discussion

In the examined case, despite the known polarized Greek media system, Syriza needed to rely almost exclusively on its news media to disseminate its narratives about the MND. Yet, Syriza's news outlets are not popular, such as Avgi.gr and Epohi.gr. These facts prove that there is no crucial pluralistic coverage despite the different news media included in the study. That finding is similar to the news coverage of the Mati wildfire, another event that dominated the discourse and harmed the popularity of Syriza's government in the summer of 2018 (Karyotakis, 2021b).

However, it should be underlined that during the Prespes Agreement, the government led by Syriza seemed to have a say in the coverage of the events by the Hellenic Broadcasting Corporation (ERT), as ERT took the controversial decision of not covering the first rally in Thessaloniki despite its importance on 21 January 2018 (Tsakiroglou, 2018). As the relevant literature suggests, ERT, despite being an independent public service broadcaster, is subjectable to political pressures (Iosifidis & Papathanassopoulos, 2019).

That problematic news coverage is alarming, as it can cause a further decline in the democratic progress in Greece and further empowerment of clientelism that can play a crucial role in the democratic backslide and the form of new regimes, such as despotisms (Chowdhury & Keane, 2021; Keane, 2020). These phenomena have been observed in other countries globally, including European Union nations such as Hungary and Poland (Csaky, 2021), that have "moved from attacking the liberal principles that underpin democracy to setting new norms themselves and openly spreading anti-democratic practices" (Csaky, 2021, p. 2).

Journalism plays a vital role in securing a prosperous, democratic development, as the journalists and the news outlets hold accountable those in power for their mishandlings. Journalism ethics and western democratic principles call for accountability (George, 2018). Furthermore, according to George (2018, p. 474), "journalism needs autonomy from government if it is to fulfil its duty to help citizens hold the government to account and to inform them about their political choices." However, this is not happening in the Greek case, in which there seems to be democratic backsliding and freedom violations under the Mitsotakis' government (Kolvani et al., 2020; Papathanassopoulos, Karadimitriou, Kostopoulos, & Archontaki, 2021), leading to alarming thoughts about Greece slowly becoming the new "Hungary" in the EU (Christopoulos, 2021). Greece seems to belong to the "newly autocratizing countries" (Boese et al., 2022).

Moreover, the current paper tried to provide insights into the news coverage of territorial name disputes by focusing on the MND. These kinds of conflicts, despite their prominence, have not been researched from a communication and journalism perspective. The study revealed that most news articles covering the periods related to the recent events of the MND were recognizing that the territorial name dispute is a crucial mobilization and political tool for electoral power.

A few articles, though, were explaining how that fact is connected with the MND. Almost all of the news stories that used that frame were focused on the accusations of influential politicians who were blaming other parties and individuals for using the events concerning the possible solution for winning the public opinion. As a result, it seems that the news organizations did not challenge the dominant narratives, a finding that has been identified in past studies (Demertzis et al., 1999; Ellinas, 2010). Furthermore, the superficial coverage of a significant issue that is based almost exclusively on political quarrels and statements has been spotted again in other influential issues in Greece, such as the separation of the State and the Church (Karyotakis, Antonopoulos, & Saridou, 2019).

Moreover, there seemed to be a populist approach (i.e., appeal to the public and promote narratives against those that designed and completed the Prespes Agreement) from several politicians, but the news outlets did not accuse them of a populistic stance. The territorial name dispute and the relevant news coverage seemed to aim to provoke the public's rage to support different political sides. That finding aligns with the idea that territorial struggles are actual symbolic disputes used as proxies to realize other goals (Chubin & Tripp, 1993; Dunbar, 2000; Hayton, 2017). However, it has to be mentioned that it was quite surprising that one of the most prominent newspapers in Greece, Kathimerini, which is known for its right-wing stance and support of ND (Eurotopics.net, n.d.), supported the solution to the MND. That tendency might be linked to the fact that, except for the Greek political parties, the majority of the political parties in the EU supported the solution. In addition, it can be linked with the notion of patriotic journalism, as the newspaper could believe that a solution to the MND could be more beneficial for Greece than a non-solution, as patriotic journalism "keeps in mind what citizens need to know to make educated decisions for self-governance" (Ginosar, 2015, p. 292).

Concerning the existential threat frame, there is no surprise that several news articles were promoting this idea, as an existential threat can justify extreme measures that can be adopted for dealing with the threat along with the provocation of powerful emotions that can shape a consensus amongst the government or state officials and the public (Balzacq, 2005; Buzan et al., 1998).

As a result, both parties, but mostly the ND, seemed to use the existential threat to protect its actions. The then-government used it to win public opinion and to realize the "Prespes Agreement" without a major decline in its electoral power. Nevertheless, that frame seemed to be employed mostly by the right-wing parties and politicians, such as ND, to empower themselves and to lead to the fall of the government and an easy win in the national and local elections in 2019. The news outlets that were using that frame are believed to maintain a closer connection with the ND. A similar approach has been observed in another influential topic of that electoral period, the wildfire of Mati, in which there was coverage that supported ND (Karyotakis, 2021b).

In all the frames of the current paper, the news articles that were in favor of Syriza were almost exclusively coming from the party's news media. The promotion of frames that were against the then-government might be associated with the notion of nationalistic journalism, as the journalists that exercise that type of journalism tend to repeat the information and ideas that are promoted by the most powerful actor in the political system (Erjavec & Volčič, 2007; Ginosar, 2015). In the examined case, ND is the most influential party in Greece and had governed the country several times compared to Syriza that from a small party, formed a coalition government in 2015. These findings are also associated with the Greek media system, which is known for polarization, low professionalism, and not focusing on its watchdog role. In Greece, there are strong connections between influential politicians and the news media (Hallin & Mancini, 2004; Papathanassopoulos, 2017).

Similarly, the nationalistic frame was employed almost exclusively by the politicians and the news organizations that were against the then-government and the possible solution to the MND. Their main goal seemed to be the preservation of the Greek nationalistic narrative for Macedonia's Greekness and to support those voices that were against the solution. The emotion of fear promoted by the nationalistic and the existential frame is based on the idea that one group is better than the other and it has to protect these unique characteristics. Otherwise, the losses can undermine the group's superiority (Baycroft, 2005; Handman, 1921).

Contrary to the nationalistic frame, the news outlets supporting or owned by the then-government disseminated the idea that their stance was not related to nationalism. The promoted solution was an act of patriotism as the "Prespes

Agreement" was securing the country's national interests that were not protected by the former governments or the parties rooting for a non-solution to the MND. Like nationalistic journalism, "patriotic journalistic behavior can be found in the coverage of any type and size of national or ethnic confrontation or crisis" (Ginosar & Cohen, 2019, p. 15). However, as mentioned above, patriotic journalism tries to educate and inform the citizens instead of reproducing dominant narratives like nationalistic journalism (Erjavec & Volčič, 2007; Ginosar & Cohen, 2019).

In addition, along with patriotism, there was a promotion of the viewpoint that the solution was a peaceful act that will benefit Greece and the EU, and the Balkans. Therefore, the "Prespes Agreement" should also be perceived as an international affair that aims to empower Greece at an international level. However, the international affair was not promoted by every news organization as a positive frame, as it was believed that the solution for the name dispute was imposed by other powerful countries, such as Germany and the USA, and, thus, it was undermining Greece's sovereignty and role in the Balkans and the EU. The idea for the foreign countries that want to undermine Greece's power is associated with the country's ideological narrative that reproduces the viewpoint that Greece is maintaining its existence by its endurance against external threats and forces (Avdela, 2000).

Conclusions and limitations

The current paper shows that the news coverage of the events associated with the "Prespes Agreement" was not critical of the powerful political actors using the MND to promote their own agenda. The news media were not in the ideological battle over the MND, as they supported the narratives mainly from the country's two big parties, Syriza and ND. If we take a closer look, the paper reveals that the majority of the most prominent news outlets from the 127 that the study included, except Kathimerini, that are branding themselves as independent (i.e., not belonging to the parties or the state) are actually lining toward the ND and Kyriakos Mitsotakis.

The paper studied 615 news stories in three different periods from 127 news outlets in order to provide a bigger picture of the news coverage regarding the MND and the Prespes Agreement. It identified four dominant news frames through a qualitative approach. The news stories were framing the Prespes Agreement and its relevant events as a political and mobilization tool for winning electoral power, as an existential threat for Greece, as a patriotic act that goes against Greek nationalism (or the opposite), and as an international affair that promotes peace or an agreement that is imposed by the more powerful nations to Greece. Apart from these frames, the absence of frames that explain the viewpoints of North Macedonia about the Prespes Agreement should be highlighted.

Moreover, the current paper revealed that in the coverage of a name dispute, such as the MND, the journalists tend to follow nationalistic arguments and narratives that do not support the journalistic ideals of holding those in power accountable or offering various viewpoints for such a controversial issue. That pattern might be similar in other name disputes across the globe, as such conflicts are usually around competing for narratives that promote a dominant truth.

Regarding the limitations of this study, the current paper focused on the MND to explore its framing through a qualitative framing analysis. Also, it tried to investigate every possible news story and news outlet in Greece based on Google Search to provide a big picture of the media content of that period in three different periods. Other research methods with different study periods can offer other insights into the incidents related to the "Prespes Agreement." Furthermore, a quantitative framing analysis could possibly shed light on other aspects of the "Prespes Agreement" events. Finally, the investigation of several other similar territorial name disputes can provide more insights and common news patterns. Subsequently, future studies can focus more closely on examining the communication that takes place during the territorial name disputes exploiting a plethora of quantitative and qualitative methods.

Acknowledgments

The author wants to thank the editors of the special issue for their efforts.

Disclosure statement

No potential conflict of interest was reported by the author(s).

ORCID

Minos-Athanasios Karyotakis http://orcid.org/0000-0002-5197-9445

References

Amna.gr. (2019, June 30). Katrougalos: Revelations about Karamanlis' letter highlight ND's hypocrisy over prespes. Retrieved from https://www.amna.gr/en/article/373365/Katrougalos-Revelations-about-Karamanlis-letter-highlight-NDs-hypocrisy-over-Prespes

Anderson, B. (2016). *Imagined communities: Reflections on the origin and spread of nationalism* (Revised ed.). London, UK: Verso.

Antonopoulos, P. (2020, October 24). "Artsakh is Armenia": Solidarity signs begin appearing in Australia's most Greek suburb. Retrieved from https://greekcitytimes.com/2020/10/15/artsakh-is-armenia-solidarity-signs-begin-appearing-in-australias-most-greek-suburb/

Antonopoulos, P. (2020b). Pan-Macedonian Union denounces government's inaction on the prespa agreement. Retrieved from https://greekcitytimes.com/2020/05/28/pan-macedonian-union-denounces-governments-inaction-on-the-prespa-agreement/

Arcadiaportal.gr. (2019, July 5). Papailiou: We have kept our commitments, we are moving forward in the fair social development of the country (In Greek). Retrieved from https://www.arcadiaportal.gr/news/papailioy-tirisame-tis-desmeyseis-mas-prohorame-sti-dikaii-koinonika-anaptyxi-tis-horas-picsvid

Avdela, E. (2000). The teaching of history in Greece. *Journal of Modern Greek Studies*, *18*(2), 239–253. doi:10.1353/mgs.2000.0025

Avgi.gr. (2018, January 28). The beginning has been made; the difficult continuation is pending (In Greek). Retrieved from https://www.avgi.gr/politiki/265350_egine-i-arhi-ekkremei-i-dyskoli-syneheia

Balzacq, T. (2005). The three faces of securitization: Political agency, audience and context. *European Journal of International Relations*, *11*(2), 171–201. doi:10.1177/1354066105052960

Baycroft, T. (2005). *Nationalism in Europe 1789-1945*. Cambridge; New Yor, UK: Cambridge University Press.

Boese, V. A., Alizada, N., Lundstedt, M., Morrison, K., Natsika, N., Sato, Y., ... Lindberg, S. I. (2022). *Autocratization changing nature? Democracy report 2022*. Varieties of Democracy Institute (V-Dem).

Buzan, B., Wæver, O., & Wilde, J. (1998). *Security: A new framework for analysis*. Boulder,UK: Lynne Rienner Pub.

Cacciatore, M. A., Scheufele, D. A., & Iyengar, S. (2016). The end of framing as we know it ... and the future of media effects. *Mass Communication and Society*, *19*(1), 7–23. doi:10.1080/15205436.2015.1068811

Cfr.org. (2020, October 23). *Global conflict tracker: Nagorno-Karabakh conflict*. Retrieved from https://www.cfr.org/global-conflict-tracker/conflict/nagorno-karabakh-conflict

Chowdhury, D. R., & Keane, J. (2021). To kill a democracy: India's passage to despotism. *Oxford University Press*. Retrieved from https://doi.org/10.1093/oso/9780198848608.001.0001

Christopoulos, D. (2021, May 7). *Could Greece turn into another Hungary?* Retrieved from https://www.opendemocracy.net/en/can-europe-make-it/could-greece-turn-another-hungary/

Chrysopoulos, P. (2018, January 22). *When Greeks rallied against FYROM name in 1992*. Retrieved from https://greece.greekreporter.com/2018/01/22/when-greeks-rallied-against-fyrom-name-in-1992/

Chubin, S., & Tripp, C. (1993). Domestic politics and territorial disputes in the Persian Gulf and the Arabian Peninsula. *Survival*, *35*(4), 3–27. doi:10.1080/00396339308442709

Connolly-Ahern, C., & Broadway, S. C. (2008). "To booze or not to booze?" Newspaper coverage of fetal alcohol spectrum disorders. *Science Communication*, *29*(3), 362–385. doi:10.1177/1075547007313031

Cornell, S. (1998). Turkey and the conflict in Nagorno Karabakh: A delicate balance. *Middle Eastern Studies*, *34*(1), 51–72. doi:10.1080/00263209808701209

Crawford, E. (2012). Them and us: Why they are nationalists and we are not. An analysis of journalists' language in relation to others. *Journalism: Theory, Practice & Criticism*, *13*(5), 620–638. doi:10.1177/1464884911431369

Csaky, Z. (2021). Nations in transit 2021: The antidemocratic turn. *Freedom House*. Retrieved from https://freedomhouse.org/sites/default/files/2021-04/NIT_2021_final_042321.pdf

Dabaghyan, A. (2011). Place renaming practices in post-war Karabakh/Artsakh. *Acta Ethnographica Hungarica*, *56*(2), 403–427. doi:10.1556/AEthn.56.2011.2.9

Demertzis, N., Papathanassopoulos, S., & Armenakis, A. (1999). Media and nationalism: The macedonian question. *Harvard International Journal of Press/Politics*, *4*(3), 26–50. doi:10.1177/1081180X99004003004

Dunbar, C. (2000). Saharan stasis: Status and future prospects of the Western Sahara conflict. *Middle East Journal*, *54*(4), 522–545. www.jstor.org/stable/4329542

Dw.com. (2018, January 21). Greeks rally over name row with neighbor Macedonia. Retrieved from https://www.dw.com/en/greeks-rally-over-name-row-with-neighbor-macedonia/a-42246009

Ekathimerini.com. (2019, January 25). Greek MPs pass prespes deal with 153 votes in 300-seat house. Retrieved from https://www.ekathimerini.com/236998/article/ekathimerini/news/greek-mps-pass-prespes-deal-with-153-votes-in-300-seat-house

Ellinas, A. A. (2010). *The media and the far right in Western Europe: Playing the nationalist card* (1st ed.). New York: Cambridge University Press.

Elliott, D. (2004). Terrorism, global journalism, and the myth of the nation state. *Journal of Mass Media Ethics*, *19*(1), 29–45. doi:10.1207/s15327728jmme1901_3

Enikonomia.gr. (2018, January 17). Mitsotakis "removed" Vasiliki Eftaxa from ND Thessaloniki - Who is replacing her (In Greek). Retrieved from http://www.enikonomia.gr/timeliness/177815,o-mitsotakis-xilose-tin-vasiliki-eftaxa-apo-ti-nd-thessalonikis-p.html

Enikonomia.gr. (2018b, January 22). Athens' Message to Skopje: Change now your constitution for the name and "Redemption" issues (In Greek). Retrieved from http://www.enikonomia.gr/timeliness/178183,minyma-athinas-pros-skopia-allaxte-tora-to-syntagma-sas-gia-onoma.html

Entman, R. M. (1993). Framing: Toward clarification of a fractured paradigm. *Journal of Communication*, *43*(4), 51–58. doi:10.1111/j.1460-2466.1993.tb01304.x

Erjavec, K., & Volčič, Z. (2007). The kosovo battle: Media's recontextualization of the serbian nationalistic discourses. *Harvard International Journal of Press/Politics*, *12*(3), 67–86. doi:10.1177/1081180X07302943

Euractiv.com. (2019a, June 3). New democracy sweeps Greek local elections. Retrieved from https://www.euractiv.com/section/elections/news/new-democracy-sweeps-greek-local-elections/

Euractiv.gr. (2019b, May 23). Anna-Michelle Assimakopoulou: Greece will have to fight in the European Parliament (In Greek). Retrieved from https://www.euractiv.gr/section/ekloges/interview/anna-misel-asimakopoyloy-i-ellada-tha-chreiastei-na-dosei-agones-sto-eyrokoinovoylio/

Eurotopics.net. (n.d.). Kathimerini. Retrieved from https://www.eurotopics.net/en/148651/kathimerini# (accessed December 27 2020).

Floyd, R. (2019). *The morality of security: A theory of just securitization*. Cambridge: Cambridge University Press. https://doi.org/10.1017/9781108667814

Floyd, R., & Croft, S. (2019). European non-traditional security theory: From theory to practice. *Geopolitics, History, and International Relations*, *3*(2), 152–179.

Foley, M. (2004). Colonialism and journalism in Ireland. *Journalism Studies*, *5*(3), 373–385. doi:10.1080/1461670042000246115

Fotopoulos, N. (2019, August 1). The "Makedonomachoi" are waiting for . . . Mitsotakis (In Greek). Retrieved from https://www.efsyn.gr/ellada/koinonia/205856_oi-makedonomahoi-perimenoyn-ton-mitsotaki

Gamson, W. A. (1990). *The strategy of social protest*. Belmont, CA: Wadsworth.

Gamson, W. A., & Modigliani, A. (1989). media discourse and public opinion on nuclear power: A constructionist approach. *American Journal of Sociology*, *95*(1), 1–37. doi:10.1086/229213

George, C. (2018). Journalism, censorship and press freedom. In T. P. Vos (Ed.), *Handbooks of communication science 19: Journalism* (pp. 473–492). Berlin, Germany: De Gruyter Mouton.

Ghazanchyan, S. (2020, October 24). What's happening in Artsakh is a tragedy: Alexis Ohanian appeals to American and German leaders. Retrieved from https://en.armradio.am/2020/10/24/whats-happening-in-artsakh-is-a-tragedy-alexis-ohanian-appeals-to-american-and-german-leaders/

Ginosar, A. (2015). Understanding patriotic journalism: Culture, ideology and professional behavior. *Journal of Media Ethics*, *30*(4), 289–301. doi:10.1080/23736992.2015.1082915

Ginosar, A., & Cohen, I. (2019). Patriotic journalism: An appeal to emotion and cognition. *Media, War & Conflict*, *12*(1), 3–18. doi:10.1177/1750635217710678

Gitlin, T. (2003). *The whole world is watching: Mass media in the making and unmaking of the new left, with a new preface*. USA: University of California Press.

Goffman, E. (1974). *Frame analysis: An essay on the organization of experience*. Cambridge, USA: Harvard University Press.

Gounaris, B. C. (2007). IX. national claims, conflicts and developments in Macedonia, 1870-1912. Retrieved from http://www.macedonian-heritage.gr/HistoryOfMacedonia/Downloads/History%20Of%20Macedonia_EN-09.pdf

Hall, B., & Hope, K. (2019, December 3). Greek PM challenges Macron over move to block EU enlargement. Retrieved from https://www.ft.com/content/c821ec3e-143b-11ea-9ee4-11f260415385

Hallin, D. C., & Mancini, P. (2004). Comparing media systems: Three models of media and politics. *Cambridge University Press*. https://doi.org/10.1017/CBO9780511790867

Handman, M. S. (1921). The sentiment of nationalism. *Political Science Quarterly*, *36*(1), 104. doi:10.2307/2142664

Hayton, B. (2017). When good lawyers write bad history: Unreliable evidence and the South China Sea territorial dispute. *Ocean Development & International Law*, *48*(1), 17–34. doi:10.1080/00908320.2017.1265362

Heraclides, A. (2019). *The macedonian question 1878-2018* (In Greek, 2nd ed). Athens, Greece: Themelio Publications.

Iosifidis, P., & Papathanassopoulos, S. (2019). Media, politics and state broadcasting in Greece. *European Journal of Communication*, *34*(4), 345–359. doi:10.1177/0267323119844414

Isidoros, K. (2017). The view from tindouf: Western Saharan women and the calculation of autochthony. In R. Ojeda-Garcia, I. Fernández-Molina, & V. Veguilla (Eds.), *Global, Regional and Local Dimensions of Western Sahara's Protracted Decolonization: When a Conflict Gets Old* (pp. 294–311). USA: Palgrave Macmillan US. doi:10.1057/978-1-349-95035-5

Kampouris, N. (2019, May 21). Greek fighter jets begin policing North Macedonian airspace. Retrieved from https://greece.greekreporter.com/2019/05/21/greek-fighter-jets-begin-policing-north-macedonian-airspace/

Kanellopoulos, D. (2020, October 16). Who altered the OPEN poll? (In Greek). Retrieved from https://www.makthes.gr/k-mitsotakis-stis-ekloges-diakyveyetai-i-ischyri-entoli-226246

Karyotakis, M.-A. (2021a). Communicating hate on YouTube: The Macedonian identity in focus. In I. Chiluwa (Ed.), *Discourse and conflict: Analysing text and talk of conflict, hate and peace-building* (pp. 203–226). London, UK: Palgrave Macmillan. doi:10.1007/978-3-030-76485-2_8

Karyotakis, M.-A. (2021b). Covering the wildfire of mati in Greece: Undermining the systemic human impact on the environment. *Journalism Practice*, 1–18. doi:10.1080/17512786.2021.1969986

Karyotakis, M.-A., Antonopoulos, N., & Saridou, T. (2019). A case study in news articles, users comments and a Facebook group for Article 3 of the Greek constitution. *KOME, 7*(2), 37–56. doi:10.17646/KOME.75672.31

Keane, J. (2020). *The new despotism*. USA: Harvard University Press.

Kis, D. (1996). On nationalism. *Performing Arts Journal, 18*(2), 13–17.

Kitsantonis, N. (2018, June 17). Macedonia and Greece sign historic deal on name change. Retrieved from https://www.nytimes.com/2018/06/17/world/europe/greece-macedonia-name-dispute.html

Kolstø, P., & Blakkisrud, H. (2012). De facto states and democracy: The case of Nagorno-Karabakh. *Communist and Post-Communist Studies, 45*(1–2), 141–151. doi:10.1016/j.postcomstud.2012.03.004

Kolvani, P., Pillai, S., Edgell, A. B., Grahn, S., Kaiser, S., Lachapelle, J., & Lührmann, A. (2020). Pandemic backsliding: Democracy nine months into the Covid-19 pandemic. *V-Dem Institute Policy Brief, 26*. Retrieved from http://homepage.ntu.edu.tw/~hanstung/Home_files/v-dem_policybrief-26_201214_v31.pdfhttps://www.v-dem.net/media/filer_public/13/1a/131a6ef5-4602-4746-a907-8f549a5518b2/v-dem_policybrief-26_201214_v31.pdf

Kostopoulos, T., & Psarras, D. (2018). *Why the Macedonian dispute is not solved*. In Greek. Athens, Greece: Efimerida ton Syntakton.

Left.gr. (2019, July 10). May spoke to Mitsotakis about the prespes, but we would never know… (In Greek). Retrieved from https://left.gr/news/i-mei-eipe-ston-mitsotaki-gia-tis-prespes-alla-den-tha-mathainame-pote

Lipschutz, R. D. (1995). *On security*. New York; Chichester: Columbia University Press. https://trove.nla.gov.au/version/25130907

Macedonianhr.org.au. (n.d.). The "Skopian" case. Retrieved from https://www.macedonianhr.org.au/images/stories/pdf/skopian_case.pdf (accessed September 27 2020).

Mazower, M. (2006). *Salonica, City of Ghosts: Christians, Muslims and Jews 1430-1950* (Reprint ed.). USA: Vintage.

McInnes, C., & Rushton, S. (2013). HIV/AIDS and securitization theory. *European Journal of International Relations, 19*(1), 115–138. doi:10.1177/1354066111425258

Michalopoulos, S. (2019, April 26). Greek centre-right party accused of 'censoring' EPP's Weber. Retrieved from https://www.euractiv.com/section/enlargement/news/greek-centre-right-party-accused-of-censoring-epps-weber/

Michalopoulos, S. (2020, September 28). Historic or not? Greece and US lost in translation over North Macedonia. Retrieved from https://www.euractiv.com/section/enlargement/news/historic-or-not-greece-and-us-lost-in-translation-over-north-macedonia/

Naftemporiki.gr. (2019, May 21). Eucl. Tsakalotos: The time of the left is here (In Greek). Retrieved from https://m.naftemporiki.gr/story/1477861

Neiger, M., & Rimmer-Tsory, K. (2012). The war that wasn't on the news: 'In-group nationalism' and 'out-group nationalism' in newspaper supplements. *Journalism*. doi:10.1177/1464884912453281

Olesen, T. (2015). *Global injustice symbols and social movements*. Houndsmills, Basingstoke, Hampshire; New York, NY: Palgrave Macmillan.

Pan, Z., & Kosicki, G. M. (1993). Framing analysis: An approach to news discourse. *Political Communication, 10*(1), 55–75. doi:10.1080/10584609.1993.9962963

Papathanassopoulos, S. (2017). Greece: A continuous interplay between media and politicians. In P. Bajomi-Lázár (Ed.), *Media in third-wave democracies: Southern and Central/Eastern Europe in a Comparative perspective* (pp. 75–89). Budapest, Hungary: L'Harmattan.

Papathanassopoulos, S., Karadimitriou, A., Kostopoulos, C., & Archontaki, I. (2021). Greece: Media concen-tration and independent journalism between austerity and digital disruption. In J. Trappel & T. Tomaz (Eds.), *The media for democracy monitor 2021: How leading news media survive digital transformation* (Vol. 2, pp. 177–230). Nordicom, Sweden: University of Gothenburg. doi:10.48335/9789188855428-5

Parapolitika.gr. (2019, May 20). Tsipras proposes a solution for the Skopjan issue to Merkel – The Surprise and the reference to Samaras (In Greek). Retrieved from https://www.parapolitika.gr/politiki/article/1000054/o-tsipras-proteine-ti-lusi-tou-skopianou-sti-merkel-i-ekplixi-kai-i-anafora-ston-samara/

Petropoulou, M. (2019, July 5). Synthia Sapika: To create a state foreign language department at the Aristotle University of Thessaloniki (In Greek). Retrieved from https://www.thestival.gr/eidiseis/vouleutikes-ekloges/463254-synthia-sapika-na-dimiourgithei-kratiko-ksenoglosso-tmima-sto-aristoteleio-panepistimio-thessalonikis/

Smith, A. D. (2010). *Nationalism: Theory, ideology, history* (2nd ed.). Cambridge, UK: Polity.

Stivas, D. (2021). Greece's response to the European refugee crisis: A tale of two securitizations. *Mediterranean Politics*, 1–24. doi:10.1080/13629395.2021.1902198

Stivas, D., & Smith, N. R. (2020, March 11). Coronavirus: China's attempts to contain the outbreak has given it new levels of state power. Retrieved from https://theconversation.com/coronavirus-chinas-attempts-to-contain-the-outbreak-has-given-it-new-levels-of-state-power-133285

Thenationalnews.com. (2019, May 27). Greek PM calls for early election after EU election defeat. Retrieved from https://www.thenationalnews.com/world/europe/greek-pm-calls-for-early-election-after-eu-election-defeat-1.866541

Tovima.gr. (2019, July 3). Stavros Kalafatis: The country cannot stand even an hour of lack of governance (In Greek). Retrieved from https://www.tovima.gr/2019/07/03/politics/stayros-kalafatis-i-xora-den-antexei-oute-mia-ora-keno-eksousias/

Trtworld.com. (2020, October 25). Erdogan warns of Europe's self-destructive Islamophobia. Retrieved from https://www.trtworld.com/turkey/erdogan-warns-of-europe-s-self-destructive-islamophobia-40865

Tsakiroglou, B. (2018, January 22). Rally for Macedonia: Rage on twitter against government and ERT (In Greek). Retrieved from https://www.protothema.gr/greece/article/752858/sullalitirio-gia-makedonia-orgi-sto-twitter-enadion-kuvernisis-kai-ert-/

Vankovska, B. (2020). Geopolitics of the prespa agreement: Background and after-effects. *Journal of Balkan and near Eastern Studies*, 22(3), 343–371. doi:10.1080/19448953.2020.1739880

Waal, T. (2010). Remaking the Nagorno-Karabakh peace process. *Survival*, 52(4), 159–176. doi:10.1080/00396338.2010.506830

Winrow, G. M. (2009). *Turkey, Russia and the Caucasus: Common and diverging interests*. London, UK: Chatham House.

Yorgason, E. (2017). Eastern Asia's revitalization of the state ideal through maritime territorial disputes. *Political Geography*, 61, 203–214. doi:10.1016/j.polgeo.2017.09.012

Zelizer, B. (2017). *What journalism could be* (1st ed.). Cambridge, UK: Polity.

Appendix

Table A1. The study's news outlets and their articles in alphabetic order.

Name of the News Outlet	Number of Articles
902.gr	1
Agonaskritis.gr	1
Agrinionews.gr	3
Aixmi.gr	4
Alfavita.gr	1
Anexartitos.gr	1
Aplhafreepress.gr	1
Arcadiaportal.gr	2
Athensvoice.gr	8
Avgi.gr	26
Capital.gr	19
Cnn.gr	10
Contra.gr	2
Creatalive.gr	3
Cretapost.gr	2
Dailythes.gr	2
Difernews.gr	2
Dikaiologitika.gr	8
Documentonews.gr	12
Dw.com	5
Economico.gr	1
Efsyn.gr	15
E-grammes.gr	1
Ekirikas.com	2
El.gr	2
Eleftheria.gr	3
Eleftheriaonline.gr	1
Eleftherostypos.gr	2
Empisteutiko.gr	1
Enikonomia.gr	19
Enikos.gr	12
Epiloges.tv	1
Epixirimatias.gr	2
Epohi.gr	3
Eproodos.gr	1
Ermisnews.gr	1
Ert.gr	5
Ethnos.gr	10
Euractiv.gr	3
Euro2day.gr	16
Euronews.gr	4
Europost.gr	1
Flashnews.gr	1
Gargalianoionline.gr	1
Gazzetta.gr	1
Haniotika-nea.gr	3
Huffingtonpost.gr	9
Iefimerida.gr	15
Ilialive.gr	1
Imerisia-ver.gr	1
In.gr	10
Inboxnews.gr	2
Indicator.gr	2
Insider.gr	9
Kalamatajournal.gr	2
Kathimerini.gr	36
Kavalapost.gr	1

(Continued)

Table A1. (Continued).

Name of the News Outlet	Number of Articles
Kefalonitikanea.gr	1
Kourdistoportokali.com	1
Kozan.gr	3
Kozanilife.gr	1
Liberal.gr	2
Lifo.gr	12
Lykavitos.gr	1
Madata.gr	5
Makthes.gr	9
Mikrometoxos.gr	1
Mononews.gr	1
Naftemporiki.gr	22
Neakriti.gr	1
Neoskosmos.com	3
Newpost.gr	13
News.gr	6
News247.gr	6
Newsbeast.gr	5
Newsbomb.gr	4
Newsit.gr	4
Newspost.gr	1
Offsite.com.cy	4
Pagenews.gr	1
Parallaximag.gr	3
Parapolitika.gr	5
Paraskhnio.gr	2
Paratiritis-news.gr	2
Paron.gr	2
Patrasevents.gr	2
Pellanews.gr	4
Periodista.gr	1
Philenews.com	3
Politis.com.cy	1
Politisnews.gr	1
Politisonline.com	1
Presspublica.gr	1
Proininews.gr	1
Protagon.gr	7
Protothema.gr	13
Reader.gr	1
Real.gr	4
Redlineagrinio.gr	1
Reporter.com.cy	1
Rodiaki.gr	1
Sdna.gr	1
Serraikanea.gr	1
Showbiz.gr	1
Sigmalive.com	3
Skai.gr	2
Sofokleousin.gr	5
Sport24.gr	2
Sport-fm.com.cy	1
Sputniknews.gr	4
Star.gr	4
Tanea.gr	14
Thebest.gr	4
Thecaller.gr	6
Thepresident.gr	1
Thepressproject.gr	2
Thepressroom.gr	1
Thestival.gr	2
Topnews.gr	1

(*Continued*)

Table A1. (Continued).

Name of the News Outlet	Number of Articles
Tovima.gr	16
Tribune.gr	3
Tvxs.gr	21
Typos-i.gr	1
Vetonews.gr	1
Voria.gr	34
Xronos.gr	3
Zougla.gr	4

The "ultimate empathy machine" as technocratic solutionism? Audience reception of the distant refugee crisis through virtual reality

Zhe Xu and Mengrong Zhang

ABSTRACT
This article aims to deconstruct the myth of technological utopianism which contends that immersive virtual reality (VR) can inevitably lead to a more moral and egalitarian world due to its promises of copresence, immediacy and transcendence in humanitarian communication. The *problématique* we explore is whether existing VR artifacts, as exemplars of the "ultimate empathy machine," construct a technocratic solutionism which becomes constitutive of humanitarian crises themselves. Drawing upon empirical material from focus group discussions and in-depth interviews with VR audiences in China, Germany, and the UK, the findings show that VR may easily construct a depoliticized hyperreality of intense spectacularity and trap audiences within an improper distance, thereby reworking the colonial legacies of humanitarianism while also obfuscating complex asymmetries of power and structural political exclusion. These findings have important implications for reminding humanitarian news organizations and aid agencies that they should not rely entirely on the particular affordances of VR to gain a moral bond with the distant refugee crisis.

Introduction

The mediated and mediatized society of today is brimming with information about the forced migration and refugee crisis in which billions of people in the Global South are being forced to flee their homes due to war, oppression, or disastrous economic circumstances. A vibrant debate on the responsibility of the media and communication technology toward vulnerable others or global societal threats has intensified within academic literature and societal commentary. Especially, the recent digitally-driven transformations in today's polymedia milieu have repeatedly pressured the critical scholarship on humanitarian communication to consider how emergent digital technologies are reconfiguring the cosmopolitanizing potential of reporting and mediation (Chouliaraki, 2021; Chouliaraki & Blaagaard, 2013; Madianou, 2019; van Dijck, Poell, & De Waal, 2018).

It is within the context of this shifting terrain of debate that virtual reality (VR) has propelled out from the academic laboratory and blossomed in journalistic practice, gaining high expectations and enthusiasm in the field of humanitarian communication due to its promises of copresence, immediacy, and transcendence (e.g., de la Peña et al., 2010; Jones, 2017; Maschio, 2017; Watson, 2017; Irom, 2018; Nash, 2018; van Damme et al., 2019; Uskali, Gynnlid, Jones, & Sirkkunen, 2020). The revolutionary idea has also already caught the interest of the United Nations (UN) Sustainable Development Goals (SDGs) Action Campaign, which has produced and distributed VR Series for evoking global empathy and encouraging policymakers, philanthropic business owners, and citizens around the world to do something (give a donation), allegedly triggering audiences' empathy. In a 2015 TED talk, for example, the immersive filmmaker Chris Milk invited audiences everywhere to experience the UNVR project "Clouds over Sidra" (Arora & Milk, 2015) about a girl in a Jordanian refugee camp through Google VR Cardboard. Following the lengthy applause and cheers, Milk loudly declared that VR is the "ultimate empathy machine" for profoundly changing their reactions to testimony on humanitarian crises by its capacity to immerse the audience in various environments.

Recent criticisms of the techno-utopianism of digital innovation and big-data-driven practices are reflected in the expression of the concepts of "technocolonialism" (Madianou, 2019) and "data colonialism" (Couldry & Mejias, 2018). They emphasized that digitalized mediation may help to advance a technocratic illusion or technical hype, in which global inequities and power asymmetries are constructed as a purely technical problem amenable to a "logic of solutionism" (Madianou, 2019) rather than as an issue concerning political and economic right (Scott, Wright, & Bunce, 2021). For example, although VR artifacts have the potential to nurture deeper empathetic relationships between viewers and refugees (Gruenewald & Witteborn, 2020), they may also "defang the political possibilities of humanitarian communication" (Irom, 2018, p. 4269). In addition, Chouliaraki (2013) argues that the technicalization of humanitarianism breeds a what's-in-it-for-me ethics of posthumanitarianism among the public. The impact of such a narcissistic public or ironic spectatorship is to relatively lessen the consideration of the political factors and socioeconomic mechanisms underpinning the suffering, sustaining an apolitical and individualist conception of humanitarianism. This conception has in turn failed to convert into a more radical and egalitarian action involving political practices of global solidarity. These eloquences and reflections in recent studies provide insightfully critical perspectives for studies on the cosmopolitan potential of VR (e.g., Hassan, 2019; Irom, 2018, 2021; Nash, 2018; Palmer, 2020; Schlembach & Clewer, 2021).

However, for now, evidence of these productive reflections in VR humanitarian communication remains very much confined to a case-based text-analytical approach. A key challenge in advancing the academic debates of humanitarian communication is to also empirically investigate the extent to which this framework and the assumptions it contains remain relevant when applied to the study of peoples' everyday lives (Scott, 2014). Recent limited laboratory-based hypothetico-deductive audience studies have predominantly probed the relationship between immersion and both empathy and embodiment (Shin & Biocca, 2017) and the effect of hierarchical immersion on news experience about the distant suffering (van Damme, All, De Marez, & van Leuven, 2019). Unfortunately, we rarely understand VR audiences' belief systems, attitude structures, and communicative practices in their mediated experiences of the distant refugee crisis, and whether these mediated experiences promote the cultivation of a cosmopolitan consciousness. This article empirically fills the yet-untreated gap in audience studies of distant suffering through the qualitative interpretative approach of social constructionism.

The article begins with a discussion of the sociotechnical understanding of the unique affordances of VR. Before we conduct the empirical study, the second section identifies three contradictions that exist between techno-utopian and techno-dystopian narratives as a useful framework for discussing the critical studies of mediated humanitarianism in relation to VR. It then develops a set of research questions and the methodology entailed by our own audience study, before presenting and discussing the findings. Drawing upon empirical material from focus group discussions and in-depth interviews with VR audiences in China, Germany, and the UK, we conclude that VR may easily construct a depoliticized hyperreality of intense spectacularity and trap audiences within an improper distance, thereby reworking the colonial legacies of humanitarianism while also obfuscating complex asymmetries of power and structural political exclusion.

What makes VR distinct as a medium?

VR, as a simulation technique that uses computer graphics to create virtual worlds with realistic configurations, is a technological phenomenon that deserves to be studied within academia (Reis & Coelho, 2018). In recent years, a considerable body of literature within scientific disciplines such as computer science, psychology, sociology, neuroscience, and communication studies has described the unique affordances of VR. The concept of affordances originated in the field of ecological psychology, where it is used to describe the characteristics that the environment provides to animals (Gibson, 1986), but it has recently been adapted within the field of information systems. In this context, affordances are more specifically identified as the possibilities for action afforded to users by technical artifacts (Steffen et al., 2019). While this literature is as diverse as it is extensive, when considering VR as a medium in communication practices, it is possible to identify two main possibilities that improve activity when compared to practices enacted in physical reality: (1) richer user experiences (UXs) than any other screen-based medium, resulting in (2) new levels of emotional engagement.

In terms of the first possibility, as VR continues to seek for novel methods of immersion or "storyliving" (Maschio, 2017) that are designed to facilitate complex audience interactivity, it may lead to a richer mediated (news) experience (Shin & Biocca, 2017; van Damme et al., 2019). Of central importance is that with VR, audiences can step into a 360° computer-generated virtual environment (VE) characterized by vividness and interactivity, inhabiting a digital entity representing the news story as if they were living in the story and gaining what academic pioneers of immersive journalism have called the "first-person experience" of distant stories (de la Peña et al., 2010). This is achieved through the presence construct, most commonly defined as the sense of "being there" that is informed by an integrated combination of the illusions of (spatial and social) presence, plausibility illusion (Psi), and the appropriation of virtual body ownership or avatar anthropomorphism (IJsselsteijn, de Ridder, Freeman, & Avons, 2000; Lugrin, Latt, & Latoschik, 2015; Skarbez, Brooks, & Whitton, 2017; Slater & Wilbur, 1997; Steuer, 1992).

Immersive first-person experiences are redefining the rules around narrative structure and storytelling, which challenges the traditional linear narrative and provides a rather high level of agency to viewers (Jones, 2017; Shin, 2018). For example, audiences are invited to explore what the experience reveals and choose their viewpoint instead of passively watching a narrative unfold from outside a rectangle of glass. As Shin (2018, p. 71) concludes,

> Based on the users' cognitive processes, it can be further inferred that there is a more active role for users in VR ... the user's role has changed from passive consumer of technologically provided immersion to active creator of immersion.

Secondly, the literature on audience reception has shown that richly experiencing distant stories from a first-person perspective may result in a more powerful emotional engagement (McRoberts, 2018; Sundar, Kang, & Oprean, 2017). Even if the VR system is considered a kind of gamified journalism or as providing an immersive gaming experience of terrorism (Siapera, 2017), de la Peña et al. (2010) found that the response mechanism runs instinctively and naturally, generating emotions such as fear, anxiety, and empathy. In particular, empathy is the most critical concept and factor that frequently arises in research on VR, and it is also the most anticipated. As McRoberts (2018) explains, VR has the capacity to augment emotional and empathic responses toward those who live outside the immediate scope of the user's everyday life.

In summary, immersive technologies are opening gateways to virtual realities that might change communication practices forever (Uskali et al., 2020). Particularly within the broad practice of humanitarian communication, VR facilitates the creation of so-called "experiential journalism" (Bunce, Scott, & Wright, 2019), in which audiences can directly experience distant suffering as it unfolds. Bearing in mind the unique affordances of VR discussed thus far, we further inquired to what extent these qualities have the potential to cultivate a sense of cosmopolitanism among audiences, which is discussed in the following section.

VR and its paradoxical cosmopolitan potential

Akin to studies in the field of mediated suffering focusing on television (Chouliaraki, 2006) and the Internet (Scott, 2015), there has been a controversial debate regarding the possibility of VR's ethical potential, or the issue of whether VR has the capacity to cultivate a cosmopolitan public. Whereas scholars agree that the particular affordances of VR help in establishing a new connection and manipulating the intimacy between the spectators and distant sufferers, there is controversy over the impact of these affordances on the possibility for cosmopolitan spectators (Irom, 2018, 2021; Nash, 2018). This competing narrative plays out across a number of key concepts in critical studies of mediated humanitarianism: reality, distance, and the hierarchies of human life.

Reality

The techno-utopian expectation for VR is that it can potentially fill the gap between a real experience and a mediated experience when the audience is immersed in the feeling of being there, creating a capacity from its spectacles of suffering to construct a true-to-life empirical reality (Irom, 2018). This is precisely because the ambition of VR is to use complex computer algorithms to realistically simulate a "real" encounter between audiences and distant actors, not just allow audiences to walk in sufferers' shoes or experience sufferers' misfortune (Nash, 2018). In this regard, VR reflects a broader logic in humanitarian communication in which it typically seeks to construct a kind of "intimate relations" (Orgad & Seu, 2014) between audiences and sufferers (potential beneficiaries) and enables audiences to sit in the territory of distant others and communicate with each other. This intimate exchange is achieved through simulated transportation to the physical space of the other and a simulated exchange.

However, the pessimistic thesis generally argues that the term "reality" itself raises a series of inherent risks in what Baudrillard (1983) called the technologically advanced postmodern society organized around simulation. The reality perceived by the audience through the media is not the reality itself, but the mediated "nebulous hyperreality" (Baudrillard, 1983, p. 44), which effaces authentic experience. Baudrillard (1996) argues that hyperreality is a "perfect crime." The fundamental idea is that hyperreality illustrates a conclusion "more real than the real, that is how the real is abolished" (p. 56). In particular, in the context of VR, such a destruction of reality eliminates the reality itself. Thus, in a sense, even if VR simulates a superficially "real" encounter, allowing the benefactor-audience to enter the scene of suffering and gain first-hand testimony of distant suffering, it still cannot replicate the reality of suffering in a fundamental sense.

Distance

With distance, we refer not only to geographical distance but also to the perceived psychological distance which includes sociocultural and moral distances (Chouliaraki, 2006; Silverstone, 2007). In general, techno-utopian narratives assert that the process of "passing through the medium" (Tomlinson, 1999, p. 154) can bring the scene of distant suffering closer to audiences, leading to intimacy and global connectivity. Specifically, VR relies on the affordances of presence and storyliving to implicitly link audiences spatially and temporally to distant suffering. The connectivity has brought distant others closer than ever before, thereby promoting the sense of mediated proximity and removing the distance in a given mediated communication to achieve the desired affective cosmopolitan dispositions and humanitarian decisions (Nash, 2018).

On the contrary, techno-dystopian narratives argue that the media fails to close the symbolic distance between audiences and distant suffering, leading to apathy and negligence. When VR audiences fully occupy the point of view of distant sufferers, VR has the "potential to undermine a moral orientation insofar as it works to obscure the distance between the spectator and other" (Nash, 2018, p. 7). Jones (2017) demonstrated that intensified proximity to the mediated characters generated discomfort and a sense of intrusion into the viewer's personal space. As a result, Nash (2018) argues that it runs the risk of creating "improper distance" (Chouliaraki, 2011). The production of improper distance in the contemporary mediations that VR provides for us represents a "failure of communication" (Chouliaraki, 2011).

Hierarchies of human life

Regarding the reproduction of hierarchies of human life on which the cultivation of a cosmopolitan consciousness depends (Chouliaraki, 2006), techno-utopian narratives believe that VR can at least partially solve the problem of power asymmetries between audiences and distant sufferers. In particular, VR can potentially address the invisibility or negative visibility of distant sufferers wherein their voices are either muted or heard only after passing through ideological frames that perpetuate the existing power hierarchy (Irom, 2018).

This is precisely because the principal cultural attraction of VR is the freedom of the virtual self, and this freedom allows the audience to experience the freedom to explore the virtual world under their own control (Bolter & Grusin, 1999). Although such freedom is relatively short-lived and virtually simulated, Bolter and Grusin (1999) argue that it has metaphorical importance for our culture, epitomizing an attitude of cultural relativism that informs much contemporary multiculturalism and a friendly/tolerant interaction style. This cultural relativism inherently challenges the privileged and unequal viewing positions between those who inhabit the transnational zone of safety and those who inhabit the zone of suffering (Nash, 2018), providing vast possibilities for a more egalitarian representation of distant sufferers.

However, problems similar to those in other media will inevitably arise, that is, the potential egalitarianism of VR is a highly contingent and paradoxical dimension that may consolidate or maintain power relations (an economic and political power relations of viewing). VR's flippant dismissal of the structures of representation is infinitely oriented toward the post-humanitarian "mirror structure" (Chouliaraki, 2013), concealing the vital issue about the unequal relationship of power, because it is eager to provide a fully immersive experience that allows audiences to forget their viewing position and fully participate in simulated real suffering scenarios. As Nash (2018) emphasizes, VR, as a new media, promotes a neoliberal transformation in humanitarian communication, taking the spectator's personally empathic feelings as the focus of intervention, rather than highlighting structural inequality and political exclusion. As a result, people are not reminded of the underlying reasons of the complex chains of events behind misfortune and atrocities, thereby obfuscating the complexity of historical power relations and the hegemonic mapping of zones of safety and suffering. The audience can potentially remain trapped within the minefield of hegemonic humanitarianism (Irom, 2018).

Analyzing audiences

A thin but growing body of empirical reception-focused studies of mediated encounters with distant suffering have predominantly focused their attention on audiences in relation to television (Höijer, 2004; Huiberts & Joye, 2019; Kyriakidou, 2015; Ong, 2015; Scott, 2014). Existing audience-centric research which focuses on the emerging challenges of platformization of humanitarian communication is relatively scarce to date.

Within this context, Scott (2015), Pantti (2015), and Huiberts's (2019) studies of audience reactions to online suffering provide not only a rare exception of reception-focused research, but also a framework and signpost for guiding further empirical research. These scholarly accounts have demonstrated that there was little evidence to support the initially posed optimistic hopes of a more (inter)active, global society and a morally engaged audience (see also Kyriakidou, 2021). Rather, an essential facet to these studies is the mapping of a critically pessimistic conclusion that the audience's behavioral unresponsiveness will remain unchanged. For example, as Scott (2015) argues, concerns about what Morozov (2011) called "clicktivism" were seemingly irrelevant, because no one was clicking. With this critical spirit in mind, the present study will first attempt to answer the following research question:

RQ 1. To what extent do techno-optimistic assumptions remain relevant when applied to the study of VR audiences' mediated experiences?

In addition, Seu (2010) and Scott (2015) have highlighted that the audience reception of distant suffering is generated within a broader media context and is permeated by wider discourses about the media. Kyriakidou (2021) and Schieferdecker (2021) have further emphasized the importance of the national sociohistorical context and specific sociocultural embedding of audience reception of humanitarian communication that might have been easily neglected in previous studies. Thus, a further key question considered here is:

RQ 2. How are the audience reactions to VR use informed by their wider media environment and national societal context?

Methods

Design

Given the qualitative nature that is ascribed to media audiences as they are actively constructing meaning and interpreting media messages (Livingstone, 1998; Morley, 1992), an inductive, qualitative focus group approach was felt to be most appropriate, particularly in researching the mediation of distant suffering (Kyriakidou, 2021) in relation to the novelty of new technologies (Nielsen & Sheets, 2019). The methodology of focus groups was used on the premise that it is through the interaction of discussion that common-sense discourses are more vividly negotiated and illustrated (Billig, 2002). Researchers have to provide an open environment and neutral setting in which differences of opinions can be celebrated and discussed freely, and participants' complex behaviors and motivations can be sighted thoroughly (Lunt & Livingstone, 1996).

However, one-off focus groups still inherently have some potentially problematic aspects, such as social-desirability bias problems. Talks generated in one-off group discussions can be "contrived" (Scott, 2014) and "faked"

(Boltanski, 1999) as participants may simply rehearse dominant discourses of global compassion or humanitarian solidarity, in which the voices that tend to deviate from the norm may be silenced in fear of repercussions by the group peers (Scott, 2014). Focus group participants may be more inclined to express culturally expected views, such as politically correct answers or inconsistent answers, which precisely create the divide between privately and publicly held views.

To partially solve this methodological dilemma, we followed significant previous scholarship in combining multi-phases of audience research (e.g., Couldry, Livingstone, & Markham, 2007; Scott, 2014; Seu & Orgad, 2017). We combined focus groups with in-depth interviews by involving the same cohort of participants in two different phases of study over an extended period of time. The in-depth interview seems to be a vital tool because it can not only probe into how mediated information about distant suffering becomes embedded – or not – in people's ordinary lifeworlds (Seu & Orgad, 2017), but it can also discover an interviewee's articulated and unarticulated (often symbolic) relationship to the VR product or experience (Maschio, 2017).

Another point worth making is that most audience studies in the field of humanitarian communication are still situated and conducted almost exclusively in the default Western context (Ong, 2015). The Western-centric and (often) highly normative realm of academia has been undoubtedly productive in revealing the dissonance and asymmetry between moral power and geographical regions, and the patterns of economic and political agency that span regions of global influence. However, a plethora of Western-based national case studies may constitute a possible tendency toward "methodological nationalism" (Beck, 2009, p. 22) in that they ignore the endemic, interpenetrating, and proliferating nature of global crises pawned by globalization and the changing geopolitical situation (Cottle, 2014; Joye, 2013) and the variety and nuance in audience reactions across different national sociohistorical and sociocultural contexts. To this end, the cross-country audience study gives us the opportunity to understand audience reception of mediated suffering in contexts other than Western countries, thereby expanding analytical perspectives (Joye, 2013). Especially, in our research, China provides a representative case, as a typically non-Western authoritarian nation. China is also the fastest growing global power, and has a rapidly industrializing economy, a distinct sociocultural and geopolitical context, and a most quintessential form of government-controlled media parallelism.

Recruitment of participants

Participants for the study were recruited in a two-phase process. Six focus groups with 24 participants in total were conducted in China, Germany, and the UK between 2018 and 2020. Two groups were convened in each country, and each group consisted of four participants. Participants were recruited using the snowball sampling method (Kyriakidou, 2014). After the targeted recruitment of the first set of volunteer participants based on age and educational level, the identified participants began to introduce others to participate in the research. The focus groups were homogeneous in age and educational level to create a comfortable and familiar environment, thereby facilitating discussions or the ability to challenge each other comfortably (Huiberts, 2019; Kyriakidou, 2014). Informed by sociodemographic data from the focus groups, and considering availability/accessibility issues, a sample of in-depth interviews consisting of 12 respondents was further identified. Four interviews were convened in each country.

Research procedure and stimulus material

The research procedure took place in participants' private residences rather than in an artificial lab setting, which may ensure the most naturalistic setting possible. This location choice not only addressed the usual external-validity limitations of a laboratory, but also minimized the artificiality of focus groups as a set-up of a social situation. This research procedure is anonymous. The identity of the participant is encoded into a public identifier that can be used to identify the text of the generated data uniquely.

The focus groups and individual interviews consisted of two phases: (1) experimental interventions and (2) discussions and interviews. In the first stage, after signing consent forms, participants were informed that the research was a study on VR news about the refugee crisis, and they were then enrolled in the experiment for experiencing the sampled stimulus material (see Figure 1). The example used for the focus groups is a documentary called "The Displaced" produced by *The New York Times* in 2015. This documentary explores the global refugee crisis through the stories of three children. The example used for the individual interviews is a documentary story called "Clouds Over Sidra" about the Jordan refugee crisis. In this documentary, a 12-year-old girl guides the audience through the Zaatari refugee camp, home to hundreds of thousands of Syrians fleeing violence.

These VR examples can be accessed through the App With.in recommended by the UN SDG Action Campaign, which provides a branded interface for interacting with the VR project through a smart mobile device and head mount display (HMD). A researcher observed participants during the interventions and documented their verbal reactions. After the intervention, in the second stage, discussions and interviews were triggered by questions about the VR stories. As group leaders and research interviewers, the authors prepared a predetermined list which was "loosely designed around the principle research questions" (Seu, 2010, p. 444).

Figure 1. (a) A female focus group participant is experiencing (b) The New York Times VR project "The Displaced"; (c) A female interviewee is experiencing (d) "Clouds Over Sidra".

Data analysis

Data were recorded, transcribed, and translated to English where applicable. All texts have been translated by the lead researcher and checked by a native speaker to ensure the accuracy of the translation. The two authors analyzed transcripts inductively and coded excerpts using NVivo 11. Any remaining disagreements were discussed and reconciled. The results of the analysis are organized around the three dimensions of mediated humanitarianism discussed in the literature review: reality, distance, and hierarchies of human life. Our qualitative analysis largely involved clustering relevant quotations into different dimensions and looking for patterns (Scott, 2014, 2015). In most instances, the quotations that are included in the analysis were selected because they provide the most illustrative, noteworthy and representative representation of audiences' discussion on a particular subject, not because they provided the most extreme examples.

Results

There were rare occasions in the focus groups and individual interviews when participants' talk did appear to reflect instances in which the particular affordances of VR had achieved optimistic hopes of the more productive and morally cosmopolitan spectatorship. Predominantly, however, the results revealed that participants' talk overwhelmingly mirrored techno-dystopian narratives. These pessimistic arguments seem to organize mainly around the intense spectacularity, inappropriate distance, and depoliticized empathy, which we will now discuss.

Reality: attentiveness on the hyperreality of intense spectacularity

The major problem which appeared to prevent participants from morally engaging with distant suffering was that they were enthralled by the filmic and dramatic spectacularity brought by the novel VR technology to the point where they ignored the inequalities and injustice of the real-world situations. Striking examples of participants' comments included "what a powerful video" (FG4, male, China); "super cool, fantastic use of the technology" (FG6, male, Germany); "absolutely epic work" (FG2, male, UK); "beautiful narration and some lovely shots" (FG3, male, China).

The deeply enthusiastic comments above reflect a "playful consumerism" (Chouliaraki, 2010, p. 107) and have illustrated that participants appeared to position themselves as cutting-edge technology consumers rather than as eyewitnesses of the misfortunes of refugees, entirely unprovided with any moral obligation to act and any further engagement with the humanitarian crisis unfolding in disaster areas. Such a reception mode is a relatively common occurrence among young males. Findings around different age and gender cohorts do seem to dovetail with previous research on audiences in relation to mainstream media (Kyriakidou, 2015; Scott, 2014; von Engelhardt & Jansz, 2014) and social networking sites (Scott, 2015). Although young male audiences, as consumers of "entertainment cosmopolitanism" (Urry, 2000) centered on global culture, show a greater degree of media literacy or would not get "lost" (Scott, 2015, p. 647) in the digital mediated experience, they were far more willing to admit their great interest in VR as a new "commodity-spectacle" (Hassan, 2019, p. 14) machine, rather than in injustices and humanitarian crises.

We found that the primary reason why participants are passionate about VR technology while being passive and unresponsive to crisis events is the problem of "attentiveness" emphasized by Schieferdecker (2021) in his integrated model explaining behavioral (non-)response. For instance, participants overly praise the performance of the "real" interaction itself, rather than caring about who they interact with, or understanding cognitively and emotionally caring for and engaging with distant victims. According to a focus group participant,

> (FG5) I believe that VR will present us with the most amazing experiences imaginable! VR brightens my outlook on the future, and interaction through changing viewpoints via VR sounds like a fantastic potential … I can't wait for truly immersive VR that sends messages to our brains, as shown in *The Matrix* (male, 29 years old, Germany).

Similarly, in the following excerpt, an interviewee who positions himself as a techno-enthusiast and media-savvy consumer confirms the immersed feeling of being there, yet has almost no memory or comment on the content of the documentary.

> (Interviewee 6) This video is breathtaking and ... the high quality astounded me ... I can really feel that I'm there. But sorry, I forgot which country's story this is telling? It is always in Arab countries anyway (male, 28 years old, China).

In this case, the lapsing and fading of the participant's "mediated memories" (Kyriakidou, 2014, p. 1474) challenges optimistic expectations of combating the problem of compassion fatigue through an immersive experience that breaks with the earlier two-dimensional experience. This is because although VR immersion does place participants in virtual refugee camps, it fails to nurture deeper empathetic relationships and intimate relations between them and the refugees. Rather, by ending with this statement – "it is always in Arab countries anyway" – the participant normalized and routinized the idea of geographies of distant suffering "that's always happening in places like that" (Cohen, 2001, p. 189). This is also constitutive of what Chouliaraki (2006) describes as a "logic of appearances" (p. 96) in which events can be understood simply as random, as if they "just happen" (Scott, 2014, p. 15).

In summary, although most audiences in all three countries validated the powerful sense of encountering with "real" refugees in virtually "real" shots, a sense which was established by the unique affordances of VR, the new immersive medium inherently trivializes realities. This is attributable to the fact that the audience is anaesthetized by their fascination with a "high-adrenaline" (Chouliaraki, 2006, p. 128) hyperreality and immersive experience, bathing in simplistic media content without a broader frame for its structural comprehension and contextualization about the society and politics. As a result, Western and Chinese participants unanimously concentrated on the self-pleasure of the VR experience at the heart of their moral action, which constructs pleasurable and fleeting forms of ironic consumerism (Chouliaraki, 2013; Scott, 2015).

Distance: improper distance

In a 360° computer-generated environment, although the participant was able to (virtually) sit around the same refugee tent with distant refugees, the zero or too close distance eventually destroys the "proper distance" (Silverstone, 2007) that is believed to be able to successfully appeal for the distant humanitarian action of audiences. This is because VR simply urges the audience to merge with the refugee's lifeworld, thereby establishing a shared identity, while utterly erasing another essential prerequisite for the concept of proper distance: difference. For example, according to the following focus group extract:

> (FG5) The immersion had the amazing capability to immerse the viewer from an observer at first to an uncomfortable narrative participant. Incredible! It was as if I was transported there. I seem to be one of them ... We waited for the emergency food airdrops together (female, Germany).

The above excerpt illustrates how the sense of absolute proximity caused participants to neglect the fact that refugees are biopolitical figures within the framework of global inequality of political economy, thus obfuscating the difference between them and refugees generated by power asymmetries. This is partly attributed to VR's obsessive pursuit of first-person storytelling in which VR audiences could fully occupy the point of view of refugees at the expense of dispossessing the voice of the vulnerable others. In this sense, the refugees are ultimately excluded from the "space of the political" (Nyers, 2010, p. 130), where refugees' voices can have the capacity of speech to articulate notions of justice and injustice, about politics and their predicament, and to assert themselves as "visible and audible political subjects" (Stavinoha, 2019, p. 1227).

Another risk of absolute proximity is the reemergence of the notorious practice of "shock effect" (Benthall, 2010) in early humanitarian communication, because the participant is *immersed* in all directions in the "raw realism" and "plain reality" (Chouliaraki, 2013, p. 58) of suffering and the "bare life" (Agamben, 1998) of faraway strangers. This has ultimately led to the fetishization with the body in an extreme state of starvation that serves to "mobilize a pornographic spectatorial imagination between disgust and desire" (Chouliaraki, 2013, p. 58) among participants. When talking about the scene in which the masses of children rush toward the participant in "Clouds Over Sidra," for instance, an interviewee said,

> (FG3) I couldn't help but want to touch the heads of these refugee kids as they ran around me ... I was filled with guilt when I looked into the eyes of these poor children with dark skin ... I'm not sure how I can assist them, and I don't know what happened to them (female, China).

As this quote shows, the form of responsibility triggered by a sense of guilt enables a vague awareness of the plight of refugees but encourages no critical reflections on the causative relation of the conditions of this suffering. Rather, these refugee children were inevitably dehumanized as "ideal victims" (Höijer, 2004) fully reliant on "our" emergency aid or rescue operations to survive. It is precisely this social relationship anchored in the paternalistic gaze that Silverstone (2002, p. 283) refers to as the "immorality of distance," in which the audiences are fully sovereign in their agency over the "passive, unaware, quasi-human" (Chouliaraki, 2013, p. 58) sufferer.

The third risk is that the sense of absolute proximity makes the audience completely inhabit the suffering zone, thus losing the sense of "mobility" (Chouliaraki, 2006). The latter is often considered a key constituent of a cosmopolitan disposition, as it helps to "create an awareness of interdependence, encouraging the development of a notion of 'panhumanity,' combining a universalistic conception of human rights with a cosmopolitan awareness of difference" (Szerszynski & Urry, 2006, pp. 117–118). Notably, in comparison to attempting to eliminate the virtually spatial distance by the use of immersive technology – albeit one-sidedly and dangerously – VR is practically worthless at bridging sociocultural and moral distance, because VR does not lead to a lower prioritization of events closer to home. There was substantial evidence in our data corpus that such communitarianism is widespread among Western and non-Western audiences, although such comments were more frequently made in interviews than in the focus groups.

> (Interviewee 11) Actually, the terrorist attacks in Berlin or London may be my biggest concern (male, Germany).

> (FG3) Many domestic problems ... left-behind children, rural migrants, and poverty ... all need to be resolved urgently. We have too many people living below the poverty line. Caring for compatriots is at the top of my ranking of values (male, China).

The first quotation above represents the logic of shared "Western culture" (Huiberts, 2019, p. 11) in which Western participants tend to prefer more comfortable, "self-affirming interactions" (Scott, 2015) with others close to their communitarian community. The second quotation helps to demonstrate a striking mis-match between powerless victims and the incapable benefactor, which appeared in most conversations between Chinese participants, and was the most agreed upon, suggesting that domestic problems are the highest priority. In this case, the Western participants in the UK and Germany who mobilize the proximity of Western culture, as well as the Chinese participants who mobilize domestic population politics, all inhabited an ironic, isolated communitarian environment and public realm that oriented themselves toward their own communitarian concerns rather than cultivating cosmopolitan sensibilities toward distant refugees (Chouliaraki, 2013; Huiberts, 2019; Scott, 2015).

In summary, the specific absolute proximity of VR may result in three risks that diverge from a cosmopolitan consciousness: (1) the political demands of the victims were marginalized; (2) the victims were fetishized in a dehumanized way; (3) the communitarian disposition or a more bound sense of belonging was maintained.

Hierarchies of human life: depoliticized sentimentalism

As discussed, VR can help the audience to more easily empathize with distant suffering, particularly among female participants. The references to affective terms in the quotations below, for example, were symptomatic of the frequent emotional, tender-hearted responses to the visualities and narratives that were depicting distressed refugee women along with their starving and malnourished children in the refugee camps.

(FG1) It touched me very much … I am so emotional, without words (female, UK).

(FG6) So sad, so full of hope … I'm without words … I want to donate (female, Germany).

(FG4) I couldn't stop weeping when I saw those kids just now … I'm at a loss for words. I hope they are all safe (female, China).

Indeed, these quotations composed of words such as "touched" and "weeping" constitute a traditional paradigm of "pure sentimentalism" (Chouliaraki, 2008) or "indulgent sentimentality" (Kyriakidou, 2015) in humanitarian communication. However, in the results we more importantly find that sentimentalist audiences tend to push aside analysis of the sociohistorical origins or contemporary political and economic causes of these conflicts, crises and emergencies. In these particular quotations, the behavior of putting aside is supported by a phrase pattern of "I'm without words," which gestures a tremendous empathy toward the distant suffering. Consequently, the participant prefers to establish sentimental bonds and charitable emotions with distant suffering through voluntary monetary donations, mercy, and benevolence.

However, the pure sentimentalism easily suffocates fruitful action by using overly moderate methods, and by turning to superficial, impulsive, and transient morality, aimed at producing fleeting moments of emotion, which presents an overly simplistic view of sufferers and their plight (Cohen, 2001). This is what Kurasawa (2013) calls "sentimentalist depoliticization" which skirts over the political factors and socioeconomic mechanisms underpinning these crises, sustaining an apolitical and individualist conception of humanitarianism, and a "short-lived" or momentary activism. These findings, at least, empirically prove the more critically pessimistic hypothesis that VR takes the audience's personally empathic feelings as the focus of intervention, rather than structural inequality and political exclusion (Nash, 2018). In other words, VR as an "ultimate empathy machine" with powerful response-ability is a limited proposition, which generalizes a narrow vision of moral response and humanitarian communication.

What is more, such depoliticized sentimentalism or apolitical benevolence not only fails to provide vast possibilities for the more egalitarian reaction toward vulnerable refugees, but also (re)consolidates or maintains the asymmetry of power between the safety and well-being of viewers and the vulnerability of sufferers. For example, the following quotations prove that while Western and Chinese participants adopted different sociocultural scripts, they uniformly maintained a clear but highly problematic negative/positive dichotomy between themselves and refugees.

(FG2) I cried watching the VR ... well, how lucky we are! (female, UK).

(FG3) It was really upsetting and sorrowful ... I have to say that being born in such a thriving and prosperous China is the most supreme stroke of luck (female, China).

As is visible in the above quotes, the originally ethical and political encounter between participants and distant refugees is grossly oversimplified to a post-humanitarian self-indulgent narcissism (Chouliaraki, 2013) in which the participant fatalistically constructs herself/himself as a "lucky" person. What this narcissistic sensibility fails to recognize is that the public circulation of emotion is inscribed in systematic patterns of global inequality and their hierarchies of place and human life. In this sense, the findings empirically highlight and verify Irom's (2018) argument that VR itself remains a social and cultural product, as well as being subject to the constraints of ideology and power hierarchies that permeate other medium and technologies.

In summary, the prominence of VR technology has an ability to enhance empathy toward the characters and emotional engagement (Kukkakorpi & Pantti, 2020; Sánchez Laws, 2017). Female participants, our research has also confirmed, tend to engage with distant suffering in emotional terms more intensely than male participants, as has been found in previous studies (Höijer, 2004; Huiberts & Joye, 2019; Scott, 2014). However, the depoliticized sentimentalism reworks the colonial legacies of humanitarianism while it also obfuscates complex asymmetries of power and structural political exclusion.

Discussion and conclusion

At the outset of this study, it was discussed how the paradoxical capability of VR in cultivating a cosmopolitan engagement with distant suffering exists between techno-utopian and techno-dystopian narratives. First, VR relies on the notions of presence and storyliving to implicitly link audiences spatially and temporally to distant suffering, creating global connectivity and reducing perceived distances between audiences and others; yet it also enables audiences to fully occupy the point of view of distant sufferers, which may destroy the proper distance. Second, VR simulates a superficially "real" encounter for visual intimacy; yet in this case the mediated hyperreality is not an authentic reality, and its simulation does not fill the gap between reality and the virtual world. Third, VR enables an audience to experience virtually fundamental "freedom," epitomizing an attitude of cultural relativism that informs a great deal of contemporary multiculturalism, providing vast possibilities for a more egalitarian representation of distant sufferers; yet it also takes the spectator's personally empathic feelings as the focus of intervention, rather than structural inequality and political exclusion.

Drawing on focus group discussions and in-depth interviews, there is little empirical evidence to substantiate the initially posed techno-optimistic promises of developing a cosmopolitan public. Rather, the findings support the more pessimistic hypotheses of some earlier studies where a form of ironic consumerism, a communitarian logic and bond, and an apolitical pure sentimentalism are found. The results of this research suggest that although VR stimulates emotional donations and (fleeting) moral awareness, the moral simple-mindedness and lack of economic and political critiques identified by previous studies remains a prominent feature of audiences' encounters with faraway refugees through immersive VR. At least, it became clear that what matters most in terms of VR's role in fostering a cosmopolitan consciousness is not necessarily the unique properties of the progressive technology.

Our focus groups and individual interviews relied on small-scale volunteers for participation and used a snowball sampling technique, and social-desirability bias was still present in group discussions; as a consequence, our findings have little or no generalizability. However, by using multiple data sources, our research findings echo the same dynamic and logic of sociodemographic variables in engaging with distant suffering as articulated in recurrent sociological and psychological studies on age and gender (e.g., Höijer, 2004; Huiberts & Joye, 2019; Kyriakidou, 2015, 2021; Scott, 2014, 2015). For example, emotional responses and pure sentimentalism were more prominent in the focus groups and interviews with female participants, which has also confirmed gendered socialization processes (Campbell & Winters, 2008). Young male participants draw their attention more intensely to the quality of the immersive experience, thus decontextualizing the structural causes of suffering and making them apolitical. In addition, our cross-national comparative perspectives have also helped to probe how participants mobilize different sociocultural capital and "local and national frameworks" (Kyriakidou, 2021, p. 98) to respond to suffering. Surprisingly, albeit in a non-exhaustive or mutually exclusive way, we have discovered the result-oriented commensurability and resemblance between different participants characterized by different political structures and sociocultural experiences.

This is significant for the study of digital cosmopolitanism in the context of the platformization of humanitarian communication (Scott, 2015; Zuckerman, 2013), not just because it dramatically opens up the scope of the medium and technologies, or advances the turn of digitalization in studies of media and morality in the polymedia milieu. Of central importance is that the article has deconstructed the myth of a technological utopianism that believes that the immensely powerful VR technology can inevitably lead to a more moral and egalitarian world. At least, until now, VR may help to advance a technocratic solutionism, in which global inequities, poverty and power asymmetries are constructed as a purely technical problem rather than as an issue concerning the broader structural drivers of economic and political divisions.

Of course, VR should not be underestimated merely as a bugaboo of an alarmist philosophical and fictional dystopia because, if it goes beyond the goal of the "ultimate empathy machine" and addresses ethical concerns, it has the potential to play a key role in future humanitarian practice and communication (Sánchez Laws, 2017). Yet let us pause for a moment to remind ourselves that dominant mediators of development issues, such as humanitarian news organizations and aid agencies, should not rely entirely on the particular affordances of VR to gain a moral bond with the distant refugee crisis. It is conceivable that in the ultimate empathy engines that are highly praised by techno-utopianism, the audience may turn into the puppets that are controlled using wires or strings, or even the Cartesian brain-in-a-vatism of the movie *The Matrix*, and may eventually become vassals of "hegemonic humanitarianism" (Irom, 2018, p. 4387).

This is a timely reminder that we must tread cautiously with the incorporation of VR in humanitarian communication. Particularly, it is so far uncertain in what ways and to what extent the VR technology will expand in the years to come, especially since Mark Elliot Zuckerberg, the CEO of the technology giant Meta Platforms (formerly named Facebook), ambitiously announced the blueprint for the development of the "Metaverse," an integrated network of 360° virtual worlds that constitutes a compelling alternative realm for human sociocultural interaction. As humanitarian communication scholars, we believe that critically and constructively studying the possible implications (or risks) of VR in humanitarian communication is a necessary task of research, even before it is widely adopted in societies.

Acknowledgments

We are very grateful to Martin Scott, Stefan Kramer, Paul Reilly, Virpi Salojärvi and two anonymous reviewers, for their constructive comments on earlier versions of this manuscript. In addition, a preliminary version of this article was presented at the IAMCR conference (2021): many thanks to the event participants for their excellent input and feedback.

Disclosure statement

No potential conflict of interest was reported by the author(s).

ORCID

Zhe Xu http://orcid.org/0000-0001-5732-512X
Mengrong Zhang http://orcid.org/0000-0002-9402-4980

References

Agamben, G. (1998). *Homo sacer: Sovereign power and bare life*. Stanford: Stanford University Press.
Arora, G., & Milk, C. (2015). *Clouds over Sidra* [Video file]. Retrieved from https://with.in/watch/clouds-over-sidra/
Baudrillard, J. (1983). *Simulations*. New York: Semiotext(e).
Baudrillard, J. (1996). *The perfect crime*. New York: Verso Books.
Beck, U. (2009). *World at risk*. Cambridge: Polity.
Benthall, J. (2010). *Disasters, relief and the media*. Herefordshire: Sean Kingston Publishing.
Billig, M. (2002). *Talking of the royal family*. London: Routledge.
Boltanski, L. (1999). *Distant suffering*. Cambridge: Cambridge University Press.
Bolter, D. J., & Grusin, R. (1999). *Remediation: Understanding new media*. Cambridge: MIT Press.
Bunce, M., Scott, M., & Wright, K. (2019). Humanitarian journalism. In C. Carpenter (Ed.), *Oxford research Encyclopedia of communication* (pp. 1–22). Oxford: Oxford University Press.
Campbell, R., & Winters, K. (2008). Understanding men's and women's political interests: Evidence from a study of gendered political attitudes. *Journal of Elections, Public Opinion and Parties, 18*(1), 53–74. doi:10.1080/17457280701858623
Chouliaraki, L. (2006). *The spectatorship of suffering*. London: SAGE.
Chouliaraki, L. (2008). The media as moral education: Mediation and action. *Media, Culture & Society, 30*(6), 831–852. doi:10.1177/0163443708096096
Chouliaraki, L. (2010). Post-humanitarianism: Humanitarian communication beyond a politics of pity. *International Journal of Cultural Studies, 13*(2), 107–126. doi:10.1177/1367877909356720
Chouliaraki, L. (2011). "Improper distance": Towards a critical account of solidarity as irony. *International Journal of Cultural Studies, 14*(4), 363–381. doi:10.1177/1367877911403247
Chouliaraki, L. (2013). *The ironic spectator*. Cambridge: Polity.
Chouliaraki, L. (2021). Victimhood: The affective politics of vulnerability. *European Journal of Cultural Studies, 24*(1), 10–27. doi:10.1177/1367549420979316
Chouliaraki, L., & Blaagaard, B. (2013). Introduction: Cosmopolitanism and the new news media. *Journalism Studies, 14*(2), 150–155. doi:10.1080/1461670X.2012.718542
Cohen, S. (2001). *States of denial: Knowing about atrocities and suffering*. Cambridge: Polity.
Cottle, S. (2014). Rethinking media and disasters in a global age: What's changed and why it matters. *Media, War & Conflict, 7*(1), 3–22. doi:10.1177/1750635213513229
Couldry, N., Livingstone, S., & Markham, T. (2007). *Media consumption and public engagement: Beyond the presumption of attention*. Basingstoke: Palgrave MacMillan.
Couldry, N., & Mejias, U. (2018). Data colonialism: Rethinking big data's relation to the contemporary subject. *Television & New Media, 20*(4), 1–14. doi:10.1177/1527476418796632
de la Peña, N., Weil, P., Llobera, J., Spanlang, B., Friedman, D., Sanchez-Vives, M., & Slater, M. (2010). Immersive journalism: Immersive virtual reality for the first-person experience of news. *Presence: Teleoperators and Virtual Environments, 19*(4), 291–301. doi:10.1162/PRES_a_00005
Gibson, J. (1986). *The ecological approach to visual perception*. New York: Psychology Press.
Gruenewald, T., & Witteborn, S. (2020). Feeling good: Humanitarian virtual reality film, emotional style and global citizenship. *Cultural Studies, 35*(2), 1–21. doi:10.1080/09502386.2020.1761415
Hassan, R. (2019). Digitality, virtual reality and the "Empathy machine." *Digital Journalism, 8*(2), 1–19. doi:10.1080/21670811.2018.1517604
Höijer, B. (2004). The discourse of global compassion: The audience and media reporting of human suffering. *Media, Culture & Society, 26*(4), 513–531. doi:10.1177/0163443704044215

Huiberts, E. (2019). Watching disaster news online and offline: Audiences experiencing news about far-away disasters in a postbroadcast society. *Television & New Media*, *21*(1), 41–59. doi:10.1177/1527476418821328

Huiberts, E., & Joye, S. (2019). Who cares for the suffering other? A survey-based study into reactions toward images of distant suffering. *International Communication Gazette*, *81*(68), 562–579. doi:10.1177/1748048518825324

IJsselsteijn, W. A., de Ridder, H., Freeman, J., & Avons, S. E. (2000). Presence: Concept, determinants, and measurement. *Proceedings of the SPIE*, *3959* . San Jose, 520–529. doi:10.1117/12.387188

Irom, B. (2018). Virtual reality and the Syrian refugee camps: Humanitarian communication and the politics of empathy. *International Journal of Communication*, *2018*(12), 4269–4291. https://ijoc.org/index.php/ijoc/article/view/8783

Irom, B. (2021). Virtual reality and celebrity humanitarianism: Rashida Jones in Lebanon media. *Culture & Society*, 1–17. doi:10.1177/01634437211022725

Jones, S. (2017). Disrupting the narrative: Immersive journalism in virtual reality. *Journal of Media Practice*, *18*(2–3), 171–185. doi:10.1080/14682753.2017.1374677

Joye, S. (2013). Research on mediated suffering within social sciences: Expert views on identifying a disciplinary home and research agenda. *Interdisciplinary Science Reviews*, *38*(2), 106–121. doi:10.1179/0308018813Z.00000000039

Kukkakorpi, M., & Pantti, M. (2020). A sense of place: VR journalism and emotional engagement. *Journalism Practice*, *15*(6), 785–802. doi:10.1080/17512786.2020.1799237

Kurasawa, F. (2013). The sentimentalist paradox: On the normative and visual foundations of humanitarianism. *Journal of Global Ethics*, *9*(2), 201–214. doi:10.1080/17449626.2013.818461

Kyriakidou, M. (2014). Distant suffering in audience memory: The moral hierarchy of remembering. *International Journal of Communication*, *2014*(8), 1474–1494. https://ijoc.org/index.php/ijoc/article/view/2465

Kyriakidou, M. (2015). Media witnessing: Exploring the audience of distant suffering. *Media, Culture & Society*, *37*(2), 215–231. doi:10.1177/0163443714557981

Kyriakidou, M. (2021). The audience of humanitarian communication. In L. Chouliaraki & A. Vestergaard (Eds.), *Routledge handbook of humanitarian communication* (pp. 89–103). London: Routledge.

Livingstone, S. (1998). Audience research at the crossroads: The "implied audience" in media and cultural theory. *European Journal of Cultural Studies*, *1*(2), 193–217. doi:10.1177/136754949800100203

Lugrin, J., Latt, J., & Latoschik, M. E. (2015). Avatar anthropomorphism and illusion of body ownership in VR. *Proceedings of 2015 IEEE Virtual Reality*. doi:10.1109/VR.2015.7223379

Lunt, P., & Livingstone, S. (1996). Rethinking the focus group in media and communications research. *Journal of Communication*, *46*(2), 79–98. doi:10.1111/j.1460-2466.1996.tb01475.x

Madianou, M. (2019). Technocolonialism: Digital innovation and data practices in the humanitarian response to refugee crises. *Social Media + Society*, *5*(3), 1–13. doi:10.1177/2056305119863146

Maschio, T. (2017). *Storyliving: An ethnographic study of how audiences experience VR and what that means for journalists*. Google News Lab.

McRoberts, J. (2018). Are we there yet? Media content and sense of presence in non-fiction virtual reality. *Studies in Documentary Film*, *12*(2), 101–118. doi:10.1080/17503280.2017.1344924

Morley, D. (1992). *Television, audiences and cultural studies*. London: Routledge.

Morozov, E. (2011). *The net delusion*. New York: PublicAffairs.

Nash, K. (2018). Virtual reality witness: Exploring the ethics of mediated presence. *Studies in Documentary Film*, *12*(2), 1750–3280. doi:10.1080/17503280.2017.1340796

Nielsen, L. N., & Sheets, P. (2019). Virtual hype meets reality: Users' perception of immersive journalism. *Journalism*, *22*(10), 2637–2653. doi:10.1177/1464884919869399

Nyers, P. (2010). No one is illegal between city and nation. *Studies in Social Justice*, *4*(2), 127–143. doi:10.26522/ssj.v4i2.998

Ong, J. C. (2015). *The poverty of television: The mediation of suffering in class-divided Philippines*. London: Anthem Press.

Orgad, S., & Seu, B. (2014). "Intimacy at a distance" in humanitarian communication. *Media, Culture & Society*, *36*(7), 916–934. doi:10.1177/0163443714536077

Palmer, L. (2020). "Breaking free" from the frame: International human rights and The New York Times' 360-degree video journalism. *Digital Journalism*, *8*(3), 386–403. doi:10.1080/21670811.2019.1709982

Pantti, M. (2015). Grassroots humanitarianism on YouTube: Ordinary fundraisers, unlikely donors, and global solidarity. *International Communication Gazette*, *77*(7), 622–636. doi:10.1177/1748048515601556

Reis, A. B., & Coelho, A. F. V. C. C. (2018). Virtual reality and journalism. A gateway to conceptualizing immersive journalism. *Digital Journalism*, *6*(8), 1090–1100. doi:10.1080/21670811.2018.1502046

Sánchez Laws, A. L. (2017). Can immersive journalism enhance empathy? *Digital Journalism*, *8*(2), 1–16. doi:10.1080/21670811.2017.1389286

Schieferdecker, D. (2021). Passivity in the face of distant others' suffering: An integrated model to explain behavioral (non)response. *Annals of the International Communication Association*, *45*(1), 20–38. doi:10.1080/23808985.2021.1908837

Schlembach, R., & Clewer, N. (2021). "Forced empathy": Manipulation, trauma and affect in virtual reality film. *International Journal of Cultural Studies*, *24*(5), 827–843. doi:10.1177/13678779211007863

Scott, M. (2014). The mediation of distant suffering: An empirical contribution beyond television news texts. *Media, Culture & Society*, *36*(1), 3–19. doi:10.1177/0163443713507811

Scott, M. (2015). Distant suffering online: The unfortunate irony of cyber-utopian narratives. *International Communication Gazette*, *77*(7), 637–653. doi:10.1177/1748048515601557

Scott, M., Wright, K., & Bunce, M. (2021). The politics of humanitarian journalism. In L. Chouliaraki & A. Vestergaard (Eds.), *Routledge handbook of humanitarian communication* (pp. 203–219). London: Routledge.

Seu, I. B. (2010). "doing denial": Audience reaction to human rights appeals. *Discourse & Society*, *21*(4), 438–457. doi:10.1177/0957926510366199

Seu, I. B., & Orgad, S. (2017). *Caring in crisis? Humanitarianism, the public and NGOs*. London: Palgrave Macmillan.

Shin, D. (2018). Empathy and embodied experience in virtual environment: To what extent can virtual reality stimulate empathy and embodied experience? *Computers in Human Behaviour*, *2018*(78), 64–73. doi:10.1016/j.chb.2017.09.012

Shin, D., & Biocca, F. (2017). Exploring immersive experience in journalism. *New Media & Society*, *20*(8), 1–24. doi:10.1177/1461444817733133

Siapera, E. (2017). *Understanding new media*. London: SAGE.

Silverstone, R. (2002). Regulation and the ethics of distance: Distance and the ethics of regulation. In R. Mansell, R. Samjiva, & A. Mahav (Eds.), *Networking knowledge for information societies: Institutions & intervention* (pp. 279–285). Delft: Delft University Press.

Silverstone, R. (2007). *Media and morality. On the rise of the Mediapolis*. London: Polity.

Skarbez, R., Brooks, F. P., & Whitton, M. C. (2017). A survey of presence and related concepts. *ACM Computing Surveys*, *50*(6), 1–39. doi:10.1145/3134301

Slater, M., & Wilbur, S. (1997). A Framework for Immersive Virtual Environments (FIVE): Speculations on the role of presence in virtual environments. *Presence: Teleoperators and Virtual Environments, 6*(6), 603–616. doi:10.1162/pres.1997.6.6.603

Stavinoha, L. (2019). Communicative acts of citizenship: Contesting Europe's border in and through the media. *International Journal of Communication, 2019*(13), 1212–1230. https://ijoc.org/index.php/ijoc/article/view/10428

Steffen, J. H., Gaskin, J. E., Meservy, T. O., Jenkins, J. L., & Wolman, I. (2019). Framework of affordances for virtual reality and augmented reality. *Journal of Management Information Systems, 36*(3), 683–729. doi:10.1080/07421222.2019.1628877

Steuer, J. (1992). Defining virtual reality: Dimensions determining telepresence. *Journal of Communication, 42*(4), 73–93. doi:10.1111/j.1460-2466.1992.tb00812.x

Sundar, S. S., Kang, J., & Oprean, D. (2017). Being there in the midst of the story: How immersive journalism affects our perceptions and cognitions. *Cyberpsychology, Behavior and Social Networking, 20*(11), 672–682. doi:10.1089/cyber.2017.0271

Szerszynski, B., & Urry, J. (2006). Visuality, mobility and the cosmopolitan: Inhabiting the world from afar. *British Journal of Sociology, 57*(1), 113–132. doi:10.1111/j.1468-4446.2006.00096.x

Tomlinson, J. (1999). *Globalization and culture*. Cambridge: Polity.

Urry, J. (2000). *Sociology beyond societies: Mobilities for the twenty-first century*. London: Routledge.

Uskali, T., Gynnlid, A., Jones, S., & Sirkkunen, E. (2020). *Immersive journalism as storytelling: Ethics, production, and design*. London: Routledge.

van Damme, K., All, A., De Marez, L., & van Leuven, S. (2019). 360° video journalism: Experimental study on the effect of immersion on news experience and distant suffering. *Journalism Studies, 20*(14), 2053–2076. doi:10.1080/1461670X.2018.1561208

van Dijck, J., Poell, T., & De Waal, M. (2018). *The platform society: Public values in a connective world*. Oxford: Oxford University Press.

von Engelhardt, J., & Jansz, J. (2014). Challenging humanitarian communication: An empirical exploration of kony 2012. *International Communication Gazette, 76*(6), 464–484. doi:10.1177/1748048514533861

Watson, Z. (2017). *VR for news: The new reality?* Oxford: Reuters Institute for the Study of Journalism.

Zuckerman, E. (2013). *Rewire: Digital cosmopolitans in the age of connection*. New York: W. W. Norton.

A systemic functional linguistics approach to analyzing white supremacist and conspiratorial discourse on YouTube

Olivia Inwood and Michele Zappavigna

ABSTRACT
Since the 2016 US Presidential Election, extreme right-wing communities have gained extensive popularity on YouTube, spreading discourses of white supremacy and conspiracy. This paper focuses on how methods drawn from Systemic Functional Linguistics (SFL) can be used to analyze this communication and contribute to research interests within the field of media and communication studies. SFL is a social semiotic model of language concerned with systematic analysis of language choices in terms of their social context. More specifically, this paper draws upon the Appraisal and Affiliation frameworks developed within SFL, in order to understand how patterns of evaluation are expressed in language and how these function in terms of aligning ambient audiences with particular values. YouTube videos and comments about the Notre Dame Cathedral Fire are used as a case study. The aim is to illustrate how this approach can offer an additional perspective on the issues of information disorder and hate speech that does not attempt to homogenize the multiple reasons why people engage in such hateful behavior.

Introduction

The sharing and proliferation of white supremacist views and conspiracy theories have become a growing concern in an age of social media platforms which are increasingly developing into incubators for hateful discourse. Platforms such as YouTube are amplifiers and manufacturers of hateful discourse due to the affordances, business models and cultures that they maintain through forms of "platformed racism" (Matamoros-Fernández, 2017). The concept of white supremacy online is connected to platformed racism, as people with white supremacist values mobilize online, centering their whiteness (Western values) and targeting hatred at a racialized "other" (Daniels, 2009; Gillborn, 2006). This white supremacy is often manifested in the form of conspiratorial discourse. Conspiracy theories have been linked to racist and xenophobic discourses, for example, in the form of islamophobia (Farkas,

Schou, & Neumayer, 2018), or antisemitism (Allington, Buarque, & Barker Flores, 2021). This study is focused on understanding conspiracies on YouTube, conceiving of this communication as political propaganda, that is, not as simply "theories" but rather as functioning to promote a political agenda (Cassam,2019, 7).

The societal threats of white supremacist and conspiratorial discourse have become mediatized via online platforms such as YouTube (Finlayson, 2020). Mediatization refers to a process whereby the media influences other sectors of society and the behavior of individuals (Couldry & Hepp, 2013). It is underpinned by the notion of media logic, meaning that institutions and individuals must adapt their communication style to appeal to mass media audiences (Altheide and Snow, 1979; Couldry & Hepp, 2013). In this study, the focus is on how non-elites respond to societal threats that are propagated on YouTube. Accordingly, YouTube's platformed racism encourages users to adopt specific communication styles in order to mobilize others to adopt their values.

This paper explores these communication styles associated with mediatization and societal threats through the methodology of Systemic Functional Linguistics (SFL). SFL is a linguistic approach that studies meaning-making resources in language according to their social context (Halliday, 1978, p. 122). It permits a systematic and detailed approach to studying language patterns because it offers methods for analyzing language across the different strata of language from phonology to lexicogrammar and discourse semantics. A core concern of SFL as an "appliable linguistics" (Halliday, 2008) is applying this analysis to practical situations in order to address social issues. Thus, the aims of SFL align with many core concerns in media and communication studies, that is, the focus on studying social contexts and applying rigorous theoretical models to understanding social issues. This paper will firstly detail the dataset explored in the study, before explaining the SFL-based analytical frameworks of Appraisal (Martin and White, 2005) and Affiliation (Zappavigna, 2018) that explore evaluative meaning and social alignments in discourse. Results will then be presented according to the Affiliation analysis that was conducted on the videos and comment threads of these videos. Lastly, the implications of this research will be considered, focusing on how an SFL approach to studying digital discourse can aid in addressing research concerns theorized by media and communication studies.

Analyzing white supremacy and conspiracy theories

White supremacy and conspiracy theories on YouTube are pertinent issues to be studied, requiring both qualitative and quantitative approaches to identifying and categorizing racist and conspiratorial discourse, in order to understand and mitigate these issues. In order to provide an overview of the field, previous qualitative research regarding deceptive content on YouTube, has explored right-wing extremist communities (Levy, 2020), racist influencers (Murthy & Sharma, 2019), populist YouTubers (Finlayson, 2020) and conspiracy videos (Paolillo, 2018). Critical discourse analysis of YouTube videos has been undertaken in order to understand discourses of xenophobia (Asakitikpi & Gadzikwa, 2020), xenophobia and misogyny (Kopytowska, 2021) and racism (Hokka, 2021). Thus, a wide array of different communities and methodologies have already been researched in relation to deceptive content on YouTube.

Research has also been conducted at the intersection of mediatization and hateful language. In particular, conspiracy theories have been analyzed as sociocultural changes developed in relation to mediatization. For example, conspiracy theories have been theorized as no longer belonging to the "fringes of media" but rather as part of the established news narrative (Konkes & Lester, 2015) or theorized as contributing to the mediatization of conflict by government agencies (Culloty, 2020). Research has been conducted into how Russian propaganda promotes conspiratorial thinking (Starbird, Arif, & Wilson, 2019) and how Russian narratives have been supported by organizations and individuals belonging to the far-right, who promote anti-Semitism and Islamophobia (Culloty, 2020; Starbird et al., 2019). Mediatization has also been explored in relation to the "politicization" of the refugee crisis in Europe (Krzyzanowski, 2018; Krzyzanowski, Triandafyllidou, & Wodak, 2018) particularly focusing on the discursive shifts in the mediatization of right-wing populist parties, who write strongly ideological messages on social media to create "the image of dialogue with citizens and other strands of the public sphere" (Krzyzanowski, 2018, p. 79). As these examples from the literature show, mediatization and hateful language have been the focus of detailed analysis. However, as Lim (2020) identifies, media scholars need to connect with other disciplines in order to address the "challenges of digitalization and mediatization" in relation to the rise of hate speech via social media networks. By engaging with the methods of multiple disciplines regarding these overarching issues, "academically informed, evidence-based, and finely balanced" results can be achieved (Lim, 2020, p. 606).

Despite the important work already conducted in relation to understanding white supremacy and conspiracy theories, there has yet to be a concentrated focus regarding how social values in conspiratorial discourse can be identified through a Systemic Functional Linguistics (SFL) analysis that considers how these values are aligned or dis-aligned with. Whilst methods in SFL have already been applied to social media, for example, to political discourse on Twitter (Makki & Zappavigna, 2021; Zappavigna, 2011, 2018), memorial tributes on YouTube (Harju, 2016), cyberbullying on Twitter (Supriadi, Gunawan, & Muniroh, 2020) and toxic positivity on Facebook (Lecompte-Van Poucke, 2022), conspiratorial discourse on YouTube using a communing and dialogic affiliation framework has yet to be analyzed. On the other hand, non-SFL linguistic analyses of white supremacy and conspiracy theories in digital communication have been explored, for example, in relation to the psychological constructs of tweets by political extremists and conspiracists (Fong, Roozenbeek, Goldwert, Rathje, & van der Linden, 2021), the discourse of tweets by alt-right supporters (Panizo-LLedot, Torregrosa, Bello-Orgaz, Thorburn, & Camacho, 2019), and the narrative frameworks of posts by conspiracists on social media forums (Shahsavari, Holur, Wang, Tangherlini, & Roychowdhury, 2020). The majority of these linguistic analyses are focused upon automated analyses of keywords due to the large datasets these researchers are working with. Whilst this research is valuable, a focus purely on identifying keywords neglects the broader discourse semantic functions of conspiratorial language. Therefore, this study addresses a gap in the current literature on conspiratorial and white supremacist discourse, in terms of applying SFL in a novel way to social media data, by focusing on the content creators and communities who engage with white supremacy and conspiratorial discourse, and the strategies they use to affiliate or disaffiliate with others. This approach goes beyond identifying specific keywords associated with these creators and communities, and instead identifies broader discourse semantic functions to illustrate how these communities are addressed and promoted.

In particular, this paper frames these research concerns via an adapted SFL approach and shows how SFL methods are relevant to the research concerns of media studies, in particular to the notion of mediatization. This is important in order to extend our analytical tools for analyzing white supremacist and conspiratorial discourse and realize how these communities draw attention in various ways. The SFL approach detailed in this paper should be seen as complementary to the research that has already been conducted regarding white supremacist and conspiratorial discourse, with the ability for an SFL approach to delve deeper into the patterns in data already identified by previous research, for example, to studies of YouTube conspiratorial comments (Allington, Buarque, & Barker Flores, 2021; Miller, 2021; Röchert, Neubaum, Ross, & Stieglitz, 2022). Thus, this study is useful to researchers wanting to add an extra dimension of analysis to their data to understand the social bonds and rhetorical strategies adopted by specific communities. This approach can highlight the nuances in communication specific to white supremacist and conspiratorial communities to aid in the prevention of hate speech and misinformation (that will be further discussed in Section 6).

Dataset: Notre Dame Cathedral Fire

The case study selected for analysis is the Notre Dame Cathedral Fire that occurred on the 15th April 2019 in Paris, France. This case study was chosen because the cathedral fire was definitively ruled as an accident by French prosecutors despite the number of conspiracy theories that surrounded the incident. Additionally, this case study was chosen because it was one of the most googled news events of 2019 worldwide.[1] Due to this global impact, conspiracy theories about how the fire started proliferated on social media, for example, in posts blaming Muslims for starting the fire, or seeking to blame the fire on their political opponents. Just shortly after the Notre Dame Fire had started, news organizations such as Buzzfeed, The Guardian and CNN were reporting on the internet being "awash in Notre Dame conspiracies."[2]

YouTube Data Tools was used in order to source the videos (Rieder, 2015). Videos were sourced from the 24-hour period after the Notre Dame fire occured on the 15th April , in order to focus on the breaking news coverage of the event, rather than its historical impact. Some videos were removed from the dataset because they were not in English. The analysis was limited to videos with more than 10000 views. After this process, 272 videos were left. The videos were then categorized based on whether the videos represented factual news reporting or conspiracy theories and misinformation. The 15 videos that had the highest number of views and represented conspiracy theories or misinformation were then selected, with these videos illustrated in Table 1.

YouTube Comment Suite was used in order to gather comments from each video (Wright, 2019). Due to the very time-consuming nature of manual analysis, a sampling strategy needed to be created. Using the concordancing software *AntConc* (Anthony, 2014), a list of the most common words across the entire comment corpus was compiled, in order to determine if there were any trends across all the comment threads. By selecting the most common word (fire) across the entire dataset, this allowed commonalities to be discovered among the videos and to effectively compare how users bonded over certain topics. From there, 50 comments were sampled from each video that featured the word "fire." This formed a 750 main comment dataset, where 225 main comments had replies. From these 225 comments, 135 comments featured conspiratorial content and 89 comments featured anti conspiratorial content. This formed a dataset of 1154 replies that were manually analyzed in total.

Analyzing deceptive and hateful communication can present some ethical dilemmas, due to the nature of this content. Fuchs (2018) writes about issues regarding internet ethics and informed consent that are relevant to this study; in terms of analyzing deceptive and hateful communication it is impossible to obtain the consent the participants, rather the greater social good of the research project outweighs the impracticality of obtaining consent from people on social media, who should understand that their data was made publicly

---

[1] https://trends.google.com/trends/yis/2019/GLOBAL/
[2] See: https://www.buzzfeednews.com/article/janelytvynenko/notre-dame-hoax-timeline; https://www.theguardian.com/world/2019/apr/16/social-media-platforms-failed-to-counter-notre-dame-fire-conspiracies-say-critics; https://edition.cnn.com/2019/04/16/tech/conspiracy-theories-notre-dame-cathedral-fire/index.html

Table 1. Notre dame fire dataset.

Video Dataset Number	Structure	Purpose of Video	Video Title
1	Vlog with social media content	Encouraging hate speech toward Muslims	The Notre Dame Fire
2	Vlog with social media content	Encouraging hate speech toward Muslims	What They're NOT Telling You About The Notre Dame Fire
3	Vlog with social media content	Encouraging hate speech toward Muslims	"We wish more fire upon you" – Muslim world reacts to Notre Dame tragedy
4	Voice-over with social media content	Explaining an arson conspiracy	Mystery figure at Notre Dame cathedral fire
5	News report with reporter outside Notre Dame Cathedral	Reporting conspiratorial discourse about French migrants	Notre Dame Cathedral Fire: Suspicion After Hundreds of French Churches Vandalized | Martina Markota
6	Vlog with social media content, dual screen	Explaining a conspiracy about Macron	Fire At Notre Dame Follows Wave Of Church ATTACKS – Will They Blame The Yellow Vest Movement?
7	Vlog with social media content	Explaining a conspiracy linked to Globalism	Notre Dame Fire: Globalist False Flag to Trigger WWII?
8	Vlog with social media content, dual screen	Explaining a conspiracy linked to Notre Dame art	Notre Dame Paris Fire INSIDE JOB, Destroying Tartarian Art by Burning
9	Voice-over with multi-media content	Explaining a conspiracy linked to the New World Order	The Notre Dame Cathedral Fire | A Planned, Deliberate Event
10	Voice-over with live-stream video content	Explaining a UFO Conspiracy	Now 3 UFOs Filmed At Notre Dame Fire! OMG!
11	Voice-over with live-stream video bond	Showing evidence of an arson conspiracy	NOTRE DAME FIRE: Suspicious Activity on Roof
12	Voice-over with multi-media content	Explaining a conspiracy linked to Freemasons	THE SCARY TRUTH ABIOUT THE NOTRE DAME FIRE THAT NO ONE IS TALKING ABOUT ...
13	Vlog	Explaining a conspiracy linked to authorities	Breaking: "Nostradamus Predicted Paris Notre Dame Would Burn"/WW II
14	Vlog	Explaining a conspiracy linked to authorities	The Notre Dame Cathedral Fire was Arson
15	Vlog	Explaining a conspiracy linked to authorities	What's the truth abou the Notre Dame Cathedral Fire?

available. This study applies a similar philosophy to Fuchs in terms of ethical considerations. All the data from this study has a significant level of popularity on YouTube, so it can be considered as very public and already well known, meaning that this research is not contributing to the unnecessary amplification of deceptive and hateful content. In addition, as a linguistic analysis has been conducted on the data, at times, quoting directly from the text is necessary in order to highlight specific linguistic patterns. In these cases, the text has been anonymized in order to ensure that the YouTuber and the specific video they are associated with are not identified.

Method: affiliation analysis

The analysis conducted draws upon the complementary frameworks of Appraisal and Affiliation in order to analyze language according to patterns of evaluation and how social bonds are aligned in discourse. These frameworks are useful for understanding the strategies that YouTubers adopt in order to persuade their audiences to align around their social values. Affiliation is a framework for analyzing how people negotiate or commune around social values in discourse. This means that there are two affiliation networks, in order to understand these different forms of affiliating. For texts that are not dialogic (such as a YouTuber making a vlog), the communing affiliation system is used (Inwood & Zappavigna, 2021; Makki & Zappavigna, 2021; Zappavigna, 2018, 2021; Zappavigna & Martin, 2018). This system captures three key affiliation strategies (shown in Figure 1) that are further divided in sub-types:

- CONVOKING: using social bonds to form or address a community, via the use of vocatives such as *"you guys"* (MARSHAL) or by naming the specific community *"as a Christian"* (DESIGNATE).
- TEMPERING: adjusting social bonds, to modify the scope of venture via graduation *"too"* (MODULATE) or through quantification to modify the degree of venture *"100%"* (FOSTER).
- FINESSING: assembling a social bond through resources that broaden (EMBELLISH) or confine (DISTIL) its intersubjectivity. For example, EMBELLISHING opens the bond to other possibilities *"I'm not sure"*, in contrast, DISTILLING limits the range, often to only one choice *"it wasn't"*.

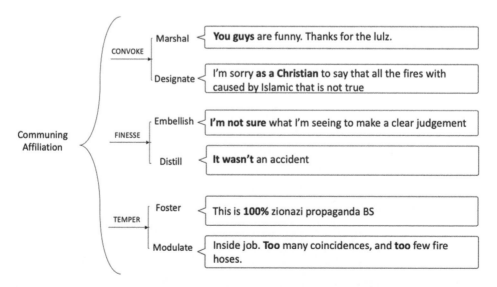

Figure 1. Communing Affiliation System (adapted from Zappavigna, 2018).

Dialogic affiliation is an interactive process where users support, reject or laugh off particular bonds (Zappavigna, 2018). More specifically, the dialogic affiliation systems consists of six main sub-types: RALLY (agreeing with the bond proposed and providing no alternatives), ADJUST (agreeing with the bond proposed but providing another bond in response), DEFER (laughing off the bond that was shared), DISMISS (disagreeing with the proposed bond and providing no alternative bond), OPPOSE (disagreeing with the proposed bond and providing an alternative bond) and IGNORE (completely ignoring the proposed bond) (Zappavigna, 2018). The dialogic affiliation system with examples is illustrated in Figure 2.

The values in these affiliation systems are realized in discourse via Appraisal. Appraisal provides a way of systematically analyzing evaluative meaning in discourse semantics (Martin & White, 2005). The analysis conducted in the present study focuses on the "ATTITUDE" system. Attitude consists of three key dimensions: AFFECT (expressing emotion or opinion), JUDGEMENT (ethically assessing a person or behavior) and APPRECIATION (valuing an object or phenomenon) (Martin & White, 2005). There are also further sub-dimensions that are illustrated in Figure 3.

Appraisal is specifically interested in understanding values as linguistic couplings of ideational (what is being evaluated) and attitudinal (how is it being evaluated) meaning. Throughout the paper, the following convention is used to mark up the data for couplings of ideation and attitude:

[ideation: ≪≫/ attitude: ≪≫]

AFFILIATION STRATEGY

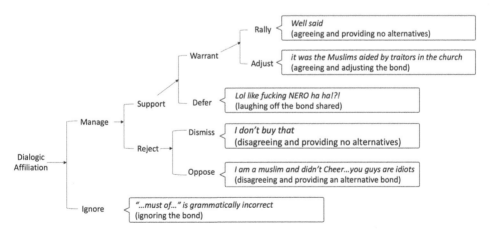

Figure 2. Dialogic affiliation system (adapted from Zappavigna, 2018).

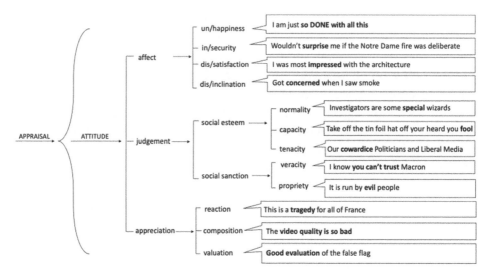

Figure 3. Appraisal system (adapted from Martin & White, 2005).

The square brackets and the/symbol suggest that the fusion of ideational and attitudinal meaning forms a value that can be negotiated through the process of affiliation. Examples of attitude in this paper, will show the attitude in **bold** and the ideation underlined.

Communing affiliation in YouTube videos

An Affiliation analysis focused on communing (refer to Figure 1) was conducted on the video transcripts across all the Notre Dame Fire videos. The aim was to identify the most common ideational targets, and the affiliation strategies used. A range of communing affiliation strategies were employed across the entire video dataset (see Table 2). MARSHALING and MODULATING were the most frequently used strategies across the video dataset, as YouTubers addressed their community as if they were talking to friends, and emphasized claims in order to make them more engaging. In contrast, DESIGNATING and FOSTERING were the least frequently used strategies, as specific communities were not frequently named and quantification was not a frequent strategy used for emphasizing claims. Most of the videos used DISTILLING more than EMBELLISHING, definitively stating their arguments rather than leaving them to negotiation. Video 11 was a particular outlier in this dataset due to its short nature and lack of speaking from the YouTuber, where instead video clips were shown that the YouTuber then asked the audience to question. Overall, this analysis shows the range of communing affiliation strategies that were used in order to achieve different purposes, in regards to how social bonds were positioned.

Table 2. Communing affiliation strategies across the transcript dataset.

Video	Total Couplings Identified	MARSHAL (directly addressing a person or community)	DESIGNATE (naming a community)	MODULATE (adjusting scope of venture)	FOSTER (adjusting degree of venture)	DISTIL (making a definitive statement)	EMBELLISH (entertaining other possibilities)
1	84	28%	5%	24%	5%	31%	7%
2	50	28%	2%	22%	4%	34%	10%
3	82	48%	2%	30%	1%	16%	2%
4	48	29%	0%	35%	0%	25%	10%
5	23	26%	4%	35%	0%	4%	30%
6	97	28%	1%	29%	5%	18%	9%
7	38	29%	3%	29%	0%	13%	26%
8	90	32%	0%	39%	1%	20%	8%
9	59	44%	2%	29%	2%	15%	8%
10	28	50%	0%	32%	0%	7%	11%
11	5	0%	0%	40%	0%	20%	40%
12	65	32%	2%	42%	2%	15%	8%
13	39	38%	0%	36%	0	13%	13%
14	32	16%	0%	31%	0%	34%	19%
15	44	18%	0%	39%	5%	18%	20%

The results across this analysis are presented in this section according to the discursive function of each communing affiliation strategy and how it contributed to the conspiratorial appeal of each of the videos. These examples will be illustrated via transcript excerpts taken from across the dataset. It should be noted that whilst multiple instances of communing affiliation can appear in the same excerpt, this section is focused on outlining the most predominant strategies featured in the dataset as identified in Table 2.

Convoking affiliation: addressing a community

Understanding how YouTuber's address their community provides insight into the type of the community the YouTuber is aiming to speak to, and how they want others to react to the key values they promote. In the Notre Dame Fire dataset, the majority of videos (14 out of 15, see Table 2) were directly addressing a community in order to make their videos relatable and persuade their addressed community to align with their values. MARSHALING was the most common CONVOKING affiliation strategy used, where vocatives such as *"you," "folks"* and *"y'all"* and forms of references such as *"listen here," "you know"* and *"you can check"* were used to address or direct communication toward a community. For example, refer to the following short excerpts from across the transcripts:

1. See Brute **was live at Notre Paris** you can check all this for yourself

   [ideation: Brute/ attitude: positive VALUATION]
   Convoke: Marshal → you can check

TRUTHFUL INFORMATION BOND

2. It is **pretty unusual** stuff so I'll play the video and you can see it

[ideation: it (fire) / attitude: positive VALUATION]
Finesse: Distil → it is
Convoke: Marshal → you can see
SUSPICIOUS FIRE BOND

In all these examples, MARSHALING is used to persuade the addressed community to align around the YouTuber's values. The proposition that *"you can check all this for yourself"* is used to support the YouTuber's assertion that the information they are providing is truthful because it can be verified. Many YouTubers in the dataset attempted to persuade their audience to align around the "suspicious fire bond" with MARSHALING affiliation as in *"you can see it,"* that presumes there is evidence for the claims made. These strategies make these videos particularly deceiving, despite the supposed evidence shown being out of context or fabricated (for example, visually in these videos, tweets would be shown out of context).

MARSHALING was also used as a strategy to garner sympathy. In the following example, a YouTuber attempts to get the audience to sympathize with them by highlighting their outsider status:

3. People to do what I do **things in their life don't go very well**[1]. You, your videos **get banned, blocked, shadow banned**[2], everything, and you cannot go out and get a public job because your name **has been smeared up one wall and down the other**[3], and everybody **believes everything they see on the internet, right, at least, they don't question it**[4], sometimes when they should but I do this **for y'all guys**[5].

[1] [ideation: I (YouTuber) / attitude: NEGATIVE UNHAPPINESS]
Convoke: Marshal → people
SAD YOUTUBER BOND

[2] [ideation: videos / attitude: NEGATIVE VALUATION]
Convoke: Marshal → you
UNVALUED VIDEOS BOND

[3] [ideation: YouTuber's name / attitude: NEGATIVE CAPACITY]
POWERLESS YOUTUBER BOND

[4] [ideation: everyone / attitude: NEGATIVE CAPACITY]
Temper: Modulate → everything
IGNORANT PEOPLE BOND

[5] [ideation: I (YouTuber) / attitude: POSITIVE CAPACITY]
BRAVE YOUTUBER BOND
Convoke: Marshal → y'all guys

Here, the YouTuber is evaluating their life negatively, for having their videos banned and their inability to hold a public job. MARSHALING directly addresses this to their audience, personalizing the video, and forming a "sad YouTuber bond," "unvalued video bond" and "powerless YouTuber bond." The YouTuber negatively evaluates people who believe everything they see on the internet. Lastly, the YouTuber evaluates their ability with POSITIVE CAPACITY for taking on the task of telling "the truth" despite personal repercussions. The MARSHALING of "*y'all guys*" again directly addresses this to the audience, emphasizing the personal element of this statement and the "brave YouTuber bond." Across this example, the YouTuber is highlighting their outside status, in terms of how they live an unconventional life where they create videos that are banned and refuse to conform to accepted notions of truth. These opinions can be easily affiliated with, as many in the ambient audience may share these values of challenging authority and promoting individualism, thus the YouTuber can successfully persuade the audience to share these views.

Another way of addressing community is through DESIGNATING that directly names the community that is addressed. Interestingly, across the dataset there were limited instances of designating. YouTuber's preferred MARSHALING that gestures to rather than specifies a particular community. To illustrate, this is an example of DESIGNATING where a warning is given to those who do not turn back to Christianity:

> 4. I'm going to say something provocative, <u>this</u> is a **minor chastisement**[1], <u>it's</u> a tiny taste of the **horrors coming, if the West does not turn back**[2] to <u>Jesus Christ</u>.
>
> [1] [ideation: this & it's/ attitude: NEGATIVE VALUATION]
>   Finesse: Distil → it's
>   TRAGIC EVENT BOND
> [2] [ideation: Jesus Christ/ attitude: POSITIVE PROPRIETY]
>   Convoke: Designate → the West
>   IMPORTANT JESUS CHRIST BOND

Rather than appeal to the church as an institution, the YouTuber appeals to an audience that is frightened about further horrors after the Notre Dame fire. "*This*" and "*it*" refer to the Notre Dame Fire that is associated with NEGATIVE VALUATION. In contrast, "*Jesus Christ*" is evaluated with POSITIVE PROPRIETY for being a beacon of hope. DESIGNATING directs this comment to Westerners, forming an "important Jesus Christ bond." This use of evaluation appeals to moralistic feelings. Overall, the function of the proposition is to convince Westerners to rekindle their Christian faith and fight against non-Christians.

COMMUNING affiliation was an important strategy used across the dataset. MARSHALING was used frequently in order for the YouTuber to persuade the community to align with their values. Interestingly, the YouTuber did not "name" this community that they were speaking to, therefore there were limited instances of DESIGNATING. Rather, the YouTubers used simple vocatives such as "*you*," creating the feeling that they were just speaking to a friend. This particular strategy could persuade the audience to align with Islamophobic or conspiratorial values, but not attach themselves to a particular group such as the alt-right. Therefore, MARSHALING was a particular effective strategy for these YouTubers to persuade others to believe their conspiratorial or white supremacist values.

Tempering affiliation: drawing attention to values

When YouTubers were communicating with their audience, values were upscaled or downscaled, as a means of explaining their importance or lack of importance. TEMPERING affiliation encompasses these ideas, in particular, how certain values attract attention. MODULATING was the more common strategy, emphasizing the significance of claims:

5. This is a **really taxing** subject and it **made me angry** just writing this out.

> [ideation: subject (it) attitude: negative REACTION]
> Temper: Modulate → very & really
> EMOTIONAL EVENT BOND

6. This is just **crazy**[1], they **think**[2] **we are really just mentally ill people**[3]

> [1] [ideation: this (event)/ attitude: negative REACTION]
> SUSPICIOUS FIRE BOND
> [2] [ideation: they (media)/ attitude: negative VERACITY]
> LYING MEDIA BOND
> [3] [ideation: we/ attitude: negative CAPACITY]
> INCAPABLE PEOPLE BOND
> Temper: Modulate → just & really just
> Convoke: Marshal → we

In these examples, MODULATING emphasizes the key social bonds that are shared, whether that is emphasizing the emotional nature of the subject (as in example 5 with the "emotional event bond") or emphasizing the suspicious nature of the fire (the negative evaluation of the event forming a "suspicious fire bond"). Additionally, in example 6, the MODULATING draws further attention to the conspiracy the YouTuber is trying to propagate. The claim *"they think we are really just mentally ill people"* negatively evaluates the media (*they*) as spreading lies to what they believe is a naïve audience, that is evaluated with negative CAPACITY. The MODULATING has an important role here in extending this claim, with the repetition of "just" extending the impact of the words the YouTuber is speaking.

FOSTERING, where the degree of venture is emphasized instead of the degree of scope, was a less common occurrence in the dataset in comparison to MODULATING. YouTubers preferred to emphasize claims through other means rather than through quantification. In the cases of fostering that were identified, quantification had a similar role in emphasizing the claims made:

7. They're **driven by an ideology**, these are thousands of people, and **this is why all this destruction is playing out**.

> [ideation: they're/ attitude: negative PROPRIETY]
> Temper: Foster → thousands of
> EVIL AUTHORITIES BOND

8. This whole thing has revealed something **interesting** about YouTube, on a side note, **thousands of videos were pulled yesterday** from thousands of different YouTube content creators

> [ideation: YouTube/ attitude: negative VERACITY]
> Temper: Foster → thousands
> SUSPICIOUS YOUTUBE BOND

In these examples, the social bond shared is emphasized through the quantification of *"thousands of."* The extent of the "evil authorities bond" (the YouTuber negatively evaluates authorities as they are blamed for causing the fire) is made more significant by signaling that there are *"thousands"* of them. In the other example, the social bond shared "suspicious YouTube" is emphasized by the FOSTERING of *"thousands of videos"* that provides substantiation for the claim that YouTube is acting suspiciously. Thus, FOSTERING also has an important role in emphasizing social bonds.

Overall, TEMPERING affiliation was a common strategy throughout the entire dataset. When YouTubers were speaking, they would naturally emphasize the particular values they wanted to promote, namely those associated with drawing attention to the suspicious nature of the fire or supposed perpetrators of the fire. This TEMPERING mainly occurred via MODULATING that adjusted the scope of venture, rather than via FOSTERING that quantified the degree of venture.

Finessing affiliation: definitive and ambiguous propositions

Propositions can be either made definitively, not leaving any room for doubt, or ambiguously, leaving the proposition open to debate or expressing uncertainty. FINESSING affiliation models these two different possibilities, with DISTILLING representing definitive propositions and EMBELLISHING representing ambiguous propositions. DISTILLING and EMBELLISHING were strategies used across all the videos, however, each video differed in their focus on DISTILLING or EMBELLISHING. Videos that predominately used DISTILLING made definitive statements in order to limit any doubt that their conspiracy theory was incorrect. For example, in this extract from a YouTube video promoting a globalist conspiracy theory in relation to the Notre Dame Fire, a story is told about the meaning behind each world war, constructing a "powerful wars bond":

9. The plan of course, the plan is you have <u>World War one</u> to **destroy the old order of Europe, the monarchies, Bazaar the Kaiser**[1], then you have <u>World War two</u> to **bring about like the UN to bring about the Jewish state Palestinian state**[1], and, and then World War three that's the **war of Christianity against Islam**[2].

[1] [ideation: World Wars/ attitude: POSITIVE VALUATION]
Finesse: Distil → the plan is
POWERFUL WARS BOND

[2] [ideation: Islam/ attitude: NEGATIVE PROPRIETY]
Finesse: Distil → that's
EVIL ISLAM BOND

In this example, there is repeated reference to "*a plan*" and a retelling of world wars. This constructs a story, connecting events together. The reference to "*world wars*" has POSITIVE VALUATION because these wars have brought about outcomes, so in other words, they are powerful. There is a lack of inscribed evaluation in this example, but Islam is still evaluated as evil at the end, with the DISTILLING affiliation strengthening the claims throughout this text by providing no other alternatives. By using these strategies, the YouTuber constructs their moral legitimation for why the West is currently threatened.

In other instances of DISTILLING, definitive statements strengthen the claims of validity that the texts are proposing:

10. These <u>guys</u> **cannot be trusted** okay.

[ideation: guys (French politicians)/ attitude: negative VERACITY]
Finesse: Distil → cannot
LYING AUTHORITIES BOND

11. Jane putting a **stupid** yellow nope sticker on my tweet **doesn't invalidate its accuracy**.

[ideation: Jane/ attitude: negative VERACITY]
LYING JOURNALIST BOND
[ideation: yellow nope sticker/ attitude: negative VALUATION]
Finesse: Distil → doesn't
FALSE STICKER BOND

In these examples, definitive statements are used to counteract authorities or journalists. In the first example, authorities (more specifically Macron and other French politicians) are negatively evaluated, with the DISTILLING making this evaluation non-negotiable. Similarly, in the second example, DISTILLING has the function of shutting down the claim made by a journalist that the YouTuber's tweet is false. The DISTILLING aids in reversing the evaluation of the tweet as false by the journalist.

In contrast to DISTILLING, EMBELLISHING opens a claim to ambiguity. This means that a claim entertains other possibilities or expresses uncertainty. Instances of EMBELLISHING were less common across the dataset compared to

DISTILLING. However, EMBELLISHING was still used as a strategy to allow the audience to come to their own conclusions:

> 12. Please pay attention. **What was** that? A lighter? A match? A welding flame? A tool reflecting the sun? A delayed-action arsonist's device?
>
> [ideation: that/ attitude: positive VALUATION]
> Finesse: Embellish → ?
> SUSPICIOUS FIRE BOND
>
> 13. So let me know what you think, **I want to hear** what people's opinions are on it
>
> [ideation: people's opinions/ attitude: positive CAPACITY]
> Finesse: Embellish → you think, I want
> Convoke: Marshal → you
> LISTENING YOUTUBER BOND

In the first example, the use of question marks, makes the statement ambiguous. The YouTuber has a range of options to choose from for what supposedly caused the fire. In this sense, the audience is given more agency to decide rather than being told what is exactly in the video shown. In the second example, the YouTuber asks the audience what their opinions are on the video. By asking "*what you think*" and stating a "*I want to hear*" the YouTuber again opens up their statement to evaluation from outsiders. In this example we also see how MARSHALING (you) and EMBELLISHING (think) work together in order to address an audience and leave a video open to interpretation.

Overall, these strategies of DISTILLING and EMBELLISHING were important across the dataset in terms of how social bonds were heteroglossically arranged. DISTILLING meant that social bonds were definitive without any room for negotiation, whilst EMBELLISHING meant that social bonds were negotiable and welcomed audience feedback. Due to the amount of hate speech contained in these videos, DISTILLING was a more common strategy as little room was given for changing ideologies. However, with videos that featured less ideology and more conspiracy (e.g. playing video clips of suspicious activity) EMBELLISHING was more frequently used, as the YouTuber would invite audiences to engage in conspiratorial thinking with them.

Dialogic affiliation in YouTube comments

This section will outline the key findings discovered from analyzing the replies to the main comments from the Notre Dame fire videos. This analysis focused on the dialogic dimension of affiliation – a framework for analyzing how replies aligned or dis-aligned with the main comments and the main social

Table 3. Replies analysis dataset.

Type of Comment	Number of Main Comments	Number of Replies (Total)	Macro-Level Affiliation	Strategies
Conspiratorial	135	905	Support	572
			Reject	22
			Ignore	111
Anti-Conspiratorial	89	250	Support	85
			Reject	150
			Ignore	14

bonds used in order to achieve this aim (see Figure 2). Replies to conspiratorial comments typically reinforced the view of the main commenter that the fire was deliberate or suspicious, with slight adjustments to the main ideational target – the specific group of people blamed for the fire. In comparison, replies to anti-conspiratorial comments, typically disagreed with the main commenter, changing the attitudinal and ideational target completely. In addition, conspiratorial comments received more engagement in comparison to anti-conspiratorial comments. These findings are not particularly surprising when considering the video dataset which is conspiratorial videos about the Notre Dame Fire. The people engaging with these videos, were already more likely share the same opinions as the YouTuber, as they belong to the same conspiratorial, white supremacist or far-right communities. However, what is interesting about this analysis is the way social bonds are constructed and the different ideologies that emerge. These findings will now be explored, by explaining each different dialogic affiliation strategy used in the dataset.

The analysis of replies to Conspiratorial and Anti-Conspiratorial comments has revealed some interesting findings regarding how the values can be mapped according to the dialogic affiliation strategies. For instance, commenters adopt OPPOSING or ADJUSTING dialogic affiliation strategies as they need to express further bonds in order to educate their audience, whilst other commenters adopt the RALLYING or DISMISSING dialogic affiliation strategy in order to "call-out" the YouTuber. Commenters that shared xenophobic and anti-elitists values could be found more so across all dialogic affiliation strategies. Commenters with skeptical views aligned with the DEFERRING, ADJUSTING or OPPOSING affiliation strategies. Therefore, from this analysis, some patterns did emerge by identifying the connections between values and dialogic affiliation strategies. In Table 3 an overview of the dataset is provided. As previously discussed, Conspiratorial comments featured more agreement than anti-conspiratorial comments, and an overall greater number of replies. The analysis and numbers in this table reflect the specific community that watches these sorts of conspiratorial YouTube videos who avoid engaging too much with people who want to debunk these videos and combat xenophobia.

Replies to conspiratorial comments

Replies to conspiratorial comments typically aligned with the attitudes in the main comment, featuring xenophobic and anti-elitist values. ADJUSTING the comment was the main dialogic affiliation strategy used, allowing the YouTube to agree with the overall sentiment of the comment (that the fire is suspicious) but ADJUST the comment to add additional bonds. For example, consider this main comment and the replies to it that use ADJUSTING dialogic affiliation:

Main comment: **A wave of vandalism**[1], the removal of statues and art, the **slow response**[2] of fire dept, **muslim extremists threatening**[3] Notre Dame, Macron is president. Conclusions made while it's still burning. They **won't look into it**[4].

[1] [ideation: vandalism & removal of statues/ attitude: negative VALUATION]
BAD VANDALISM & REMOVAL OF STATUES BOND
[2] [ideation: fire department/ attitude: negative CAPACITY]
LAZY FIRE DEPARTMENT BOND
[3] [ideation: muslim extremists & Macron/ attitude: negative PROPRIETY]
EVIL MUSLIMS AND MACRON BOND
[4] [ideation: authorities/ attitude: negative PROPRIETY]
SUSPICIOUS AUTHORITIES BOND

Replies:

1. **Just like**[1] 9/11. Elites **used**[2] Muslims **to carry out the attack**[3].

   [1] [ideation: 9/11/ attitude: negative VALUATION]
   SUSPICIOUS FIRE BOND
   [2] [ideation: elites/ attitude: negative PROPRIETY]
   EVIL ELITES BOND
   [3] [ideation: muslims/ attitude: negative CAPACITY]
   EVIL MUSLIMS BOND

2. i know where Michelle Obama was. In Paris sipping champagne while watching the bonfire and peddling her book. **Coincidence or not?**. 🔥

   [ideation: Michelle Obama/ attitude: negative PROPRIETY]
   EVIL MICHELE OBAMA BOND

3. I is CLEARLY to **WORK of LUCIFER**[1], who has The **mooooslums**[2] under his spell.

   [1] [ideation: it (fire) / attitude: negative VALUATION]
   SUSPICIOUS FIRE BOND
   [2] [ideation: muslims/ attitude: negative PROPRIETY]
   EVIL MUSLIMS BOND

The main comment lists a number of negative attitudinal targets – *vandalism, removal of statues, fire department, Muslims and Macron* as all evil and suspicious activity. "*They*" in this case refers to authorities that are supposedly refusing to investigate these negative attitudinal targets. This comment reflects anti-Elitist values, as it predominately delegitimatizes authorities. The replies to this comment share a similar opinion, that the fire is suspicious, but differ in the strength of their attitudinal targets. The first two replies also reflect Anti-Elitist values but have ADJUSTED ideational targets. In reply 1, the replier agrees that the fire is suspicious, but they add the additional bond of the fire resembling *"9/11,"* and elites being the *"evil"* people who caused the fire, with Muslims as their accomplice (in this case, Muslims has negative CAPACITY, as they are being *"used"* by elites). In reply 2, Michelle Obama is negatively evaluated as she was in Paris when the Notre Dame Fire occurred, and this replier is peddling a conspiracy theory from this knowledge. Reply 3, contains xenophobic social bonds as negative evaluation is directed toward Muslims. The fire is evaluated negatively because it is the *"work of Lucifer."* In addition, Muslims are also negatively evaluated for being under the *"spell"* of Lucifer, and for the derogatory spelling of Muslims as *"mooooslums."* From this example, we can see how ADJUSTING dialogic affiliation works in regards to conspiratorial comments – the repliers agree with the overall sentiment that the fire is suspicious but differ in their key ideational targets, the people who are blamed for causing the fire.

Repliers that RALLIED around a comment accepted the exact same bond that was depicted in the main comment. In this sense, RALLYING dialogic affiliation comments were typically constructed around the same bond – a *"good comment"* bond, expressing complete agreement with the main commenter. Examples of RALLYING replies are shown here:

```
User 1: thanks!
User 2: Quite right.
User 3: Good comment!
User 4: Extremely
User 5: agreed
User 6: Well said
User 7: i feel you
```

All these comments are short and sometimes completely miss stating the ideational target. However, it can be inferred that they all express positive attitude toward the main comment. Based on the high level of agreement, this means that the repliers are aligning themselves with the same social bonds as the main commenter.

Replies that DEFERRED the main comment would "laugh off" the main comment. In other words, "laughing affiliation" is formed when there is tension and a bond cannot be simply rallied around (Knight, 2010; Zappavigna, 2018). With the nature of YouTube comments, humor and sarcasm are frequent in comment threads (Thelwall, Sud, & Vis, 2012). As in the following example, the replier "laughs off" the main comment:

Main comment: Macron **lit** 🔥 **the fire himself**¹, this way he can blame the yellow jackets 🦺, and save France. (by the way France **is already lost**², it is in the eu)

¹ [ideation: Macron/ attitude: negative PROPRIETY]
   EVIL MACRON BOND
² [ideation: France/ attitude: negative CAPACITY]
   LOST FRANCE BOND
² [ideation: EU/ attitude: negative PROPRIETY]
   EVIL EU BOND

Reply: **lol**¹ like fucking NERO **ha ha!?!**²

¹ [ideation: comment/ attitude: positive REACTION]
   ENTERTAINING COMMENT BOND
² [ideation: Nero/ attitude: negative PROPRIETY]
   EVIL NERO AND MACRON BOND

The main comment has several main ideational targets. Macron is negatively evaluated for supposedly causing the fire and blaming it on the *"yellow jackets."* France and the EU are also negatively evaluated – France because it has no power, and the EU because it has negatively impacted France. This comment manifests Anti-Elitist values due to these delegitimations of authority. Whether the commenter means this sarcastically or if they are serious, can be difficult to tell, but we can assume that this comment intends to delegitimise authorities based on the negative bonds shared. The reply to this comment, firstly rallies around the comment by laughing at it, hence forming an "entertaining comment bond." However, in the next coupling, the reply "laughs off" the bond that Macron lit the fire, by comparing Macron to the Roman Emperor Nero who was rumored to have ordered the Great Fire of Rome. This strategy of laughing off the bond and using question marks most aligns with skeptic values that express uncertainty. With this example we can see how DEFERRING replies typically treat the main comment as a joke, regardless of the main commenter's intentions.

DISMISSING dialogic affiliation rejects the main commenter's bond and does not propose an alternative bond. There were linguistic similarities with DISMISSING and RALLYING replies, despite the different polarities, these replies were both short and elided ideational targets. DISMISSING replies were typically constructed around two key bonds, the "false comment bond" and "ignorant YouTuber bond." Replies that incorporated the "false comment bond" were:

User 1: **I don't buy** that .
User 2: **not true**
User 3: **BS**
User 4: **Proof?**

These comments explicitly state that the comment is false or express skepticism as in *"Proof?."* The other key bond that DISMISSING replies shared was the "ignorant YouTuber bond":

> User 1: **moron**
> User 2: **Nutcase lol**
> User 3: **Oh shut up**

These replies all directly target the YouTuber for their ignorance or insanity. DISMISSING replies were not common with conspiratorial comments as they were heavily outnumbered by replies that agreed with the main comment.

OPPOSING dialogic affiliation disagrees with the main comment and provides an alternative coupling. Again, disagreement among conspiratorial main comments was not frequent, but this strategy appeared more than the DISMISSING affiliation strategy. The following are examples of OPPOSING replies to main comments that were of a xenophobic or anti-elitist nature:

1. I am a muslim and **didn't Cheer**[1]. Just as many other muslims **have not cheered**[1]. You Guys **are Idiots**[2]

   [1] [ideation: muslims/ attitude: positive PROPRIETY]
   GOOD MUSLIMS BOND
   [2] [ideation: you guys/ attitude: negative CAPACITY]
   IGNORANT YOUTUBERS BOND

2. Thats **bullshit**[1], are you from Europe, or not, **do not believe everything**[1].... And they have **good**[2] firemen, because ALL firemen are **good WORLDWIDE**[2], because they help in need and they risk their lives for it...

   [1] [ideation: comment/ attitude: negative VALUATION]
   BAD COMMENT BOND
   [2] [ideation: firemen/ attitude: positive PROPRIETY]
   GOOD FIREMEN BOND

With reply 1, Muslims are positively evaluated, as caring people. The "good Muslims bond" opposes the claims in the main comment that Muslims cheered when the Notre Dame Cathedral was on fire. In addition, the people commenting xenophobic statements are negatively evaluated as *"idiots"* by the replier. This replier uses additional bonds to explain why a comment is incorrect. With reply 2, the replier opposes a main commenter that negatively evaluates firefighters. The replier instead negatively evaluates the comment and positively evaluates firemen in terms of social sanction. Thus, in all these examples we can see how opposing replies debunk or call-out what is stated in the main comment, presenting more bonds than the dismissing replies.

Lastly, there were replies that did not directly engage with the main comment, in the sense that they did not express agreement or disagreement. These replies are labeled as IGNORING dialogic affiliation. Examples from the dataset are shown here:

> User 1: **don't say** huhhhhh like @YouTuber 😒
> User 2: **Don't you mean** " . . . must have been . . . " or " . . . must've been . . . "?
> User 3: " . . . must of . . . " is **grammatically incorrect**.

What these examples share in common, is that they do not engage with the YouTuber's bonds but attempt to correct the YouTuber's speaking mannerisms or a commenter's spelling. Again, with these short comments, sometimes ideational targets are not explicitly stated, as with the reply "grammatically incorrect" that is just attitude with no explicit ideation. These sorts of comments do not align with a particular political ideology.

Overall, replies to Conspiratorial comments agreed more frequently with the main comment rather than disagreeing with it. ADJUSTING replies were the most common, as YouTuber's preferred to agree with the general gist of the comment but also add their own speculation, by shifting the ideational targets of who is to blame for the fire. By identifying each dialogic affiliation strategy, it was also discovered that the repliers typically aligned with the values identified from the main comment dataset. For example, those with xenophobes or anti-elitist values used ADJUSTED or RALLYING replies, those skeptical of the main comment would use DEFERRING replies, those who disagreed used DISMISSING replies, and those who wanted to educate others used OPPOSING replies.

Replies to anti-conspiratorial comments

Replies to Anti-Conspiratorial comments were less frequent, and hence there was an overall smaller dataset to analyze. These replies more typically disagreed with the main comment, thus there were more instances of opposing and dismissing replies. OPPOSING dialogic affiliation was the most common strategy, where repliers disagreed with the main comment that attempted to debunk the conspiratorial YouTube video, instead these repliers would add additional bonds of a conspiratorial or xenophobic nature:

1. **Nothing** in the news is **coincidence**. It's **all messages and spells**.

   [ideation: news/ attitude: negative VALUATION]
   SUSPICIOUS NEWS BOND

2. Cheap immigrant workers or Refugees and undercover agents?

   [ideation: immigrants & refugees & undercover agents/ attitude: negative PROPRIETY]
   SUSPICIOUS IMMIGRANTS/REFUGEES/UNDERCOVER AGENTS BOND

3. We **don't need any**[1] evidence. Anyone with half a brain will know who **the scum are responsible**[2]

[1] [ideation: evidence/ attitude: negative VALUATION]
   USELESS EVIDENCE BOND
[2] [ideation: Muslims/ attitude: negative PROPRIETY]
   EVIL MUSLIMS BOND

With reply 1, the replier opposes a main comment that states the fire is not suspicious and that coincidences can happen. The replier negatively evaluates the news for its suspicious nature and promotes conspiratorial thinking. In reply 2, we also see an additional bond added, the replier here is responding to a main comment that discusses workers causing an accidental fire. The replier adds an additional bond of a xenophobic and anti-elitist nature, negatively evaluating immigrant workers, refugees and undercover agents. The question mark in this reply insinuates that they are associated with the fire. In reply 3, the comment directly opposes the main commenter's discussion about evidence. This replier delegitimises the importance of evidence by negatively evaluating it, and instead launches into a xenophobic attack of Muslims, that they refer to here as *"the scum."* In all these instances, we see how opposing replies create additional bonds that align with conspiratorial, anti-elitist and xenophobic values.

DISMISSING dialogic affiliation was another common strategy among replies to Anti-Conspiratorial comments. In these instances, replies were short and directly called out the main commenter:

User 1: You are **not a Christian**.
User 2: **go get help**
User 3: **Go back to sleep**.
User 4: **Get back under** your **bridge**

Replies would align with xenophobic values and an obsession with who is righteous, thus by saying someone is not Christian, this would associate them with negative PROPRIETY. Other replies were more aligned with classic conspiratorial values, for example, being concerned with people who are not *"awake"* to their conspiracy theories, often referring to these people as *"sheeple."*

In comparison to the "Replies to Conspiratorial Comments," there were less instances of replies that agreed with the main comment. Replies that used ADJUSTING dialogic affiliation, would add additional bonds that provided an additional reason for why the main comment was correct in debunking a video. As we see in this instance:

Main comment: **Ah ah ah** the "mysterious" figure is a fireman 😂😂😂😂 if you play the video for another 5 seconds you can see the rest of the fire brigade joining him. 😂😂😂😂😂😂😂😂😂

[ideation: the video/ attitude: negative VALUATION]
MISLEADING VIDEO BOND

Replies:

1. The head fireman **looked different** because he wore a fire retardant reflective vest over his jacket. **That's all.**

[ideation: footage of firemen/ attitude: positive VALUATION]
UNSUSPICIOUS FIRE BOND

2. no link. Just shown to us **live on French TV**[1]. That's all. **No conspiracy**[1]. The internet is full of montages relayed by **not so reliable**[2] medias.

[1] [ideation: live on French TV/ attitude: positive VALUATION]
RELIABLE FRENCH TV BOND
[2] [ideation: media/ attitude: negative VERACITY]
UNRELIABLE MEDIA BOND

The main comment negatively evaluates the YouTube video for being misleading, as the mysterious figure is just a fireman. Similarly, reply 1 agrees with the main comment but adds some additional bonds to explain exactly why it is a fireman in the video. Thus, these sorts of comments form an overall "unsuspicious fire bond," debunking the content of the YouTube videos. In reply 2, the replier also agrees with the main comment but provides an additional commentary of why they don't believe the YouTube video, negatively evaluating media that is not reliable, and positively evaluating live French TV.

RALLYING dialogic affiliation directly agreed with what was expressed in the main comment, not adding further additional bonds. In similarity to the "Replies to Conspiratorial Comments" these replies were short and had minimal ideational targets:

User 1: **ok**
User 2: (YouTuber) **exactly**.
User 3: **excellent** comment . . .)
User 4: **Thanks for that!:)**
User 5: **yeah saw that**. ☺
User 6: thanks. **interesting**. it is **good to know** history before making an opinion.

These replies all featured positive evaluation toward the YouTuber or their comment. As these replies directly align with the main comment, this means the repliers are aligned with the same values as the main commenter.

DEFERRING dialogic affiliation was also evident in the dataset. In these instances of laughing affiliation, we have:

Main comment: OMG another **armchair professional**[1] talking **as if he knows something about firefighting and live streaming**[1]. <u>You should stop spending so much time on the internet</u>[2], and try to **speak with**[3] the <u>people involved in those kind of operations</u>. That might give <u>you</u> **a better understanding**[3]. **Not worth spending more time**[2] on <u>you</u>.

[1] [ideation: armchair professional/ attitude: negative CAPACITY]
[2] [ideation: you/ attitude: negative CAPACITY]
IGNORANT YOUTUBER BOND
[3] [ideation: people involved in those kinds of operations/ attitude: positive CAPACITY]
CAPABLE AUTHORITIES BOND

Reply: **LOL** . . . the Blue pill or the red pill . . . .

Main comment: <u>Two wrongs</u> **don't make a right!**

[ideation: (video)/ attitude: negative VALUATION]
FALSE VIDEO BOND

Reply: Two wongs don't make a **white**. 😂

In the first instance, the main commenter is negatively evaluating and delegitimating the YouTuber for not being an expert in what they've created a video about. Instead, the main commenter positively evaluates and legitimizes the authorities involved in fighting the fire. The reply to this comment laughs off the bonds shared, instead posing the question whether one wants to remain in ignorance or not. In the second instance, the main commenter repeats a common proverb, inferring that an allegation of wrongdoing should not be encountered with a similar action. The reply to this comment defers the bond, instead laughing at the comment by rewording right to white, aligning with white supremacist values. Thus, these instances of "laughing off" the bond have added additional meanings to the comment.

Lastly, there were also some instances of IGNORING dialogic affiliation in the dataset, but these were the least common. These instances of ignoring replies asked questions that were unrelated to the main comment or made a joke that did not relate to the main comment. Some examples are shown here:

User 1: Where would the hotwork be done on a <u>wood and stone building?</u>
[ideation: building/ attitude: negative VALUATION]
User 2: No, it have been <u>Billy Joel.</u>
[ideation: Billy Joel/ attitude: negative PROPRIETY]

These examples do not align with the main comment that was discussing the Notre Dame Fire.. Instead, they provide irrelevant information, and do not align with the values discovered in the main comment dataset.

Overall, replies to Anti-Conspiratorial comments featured more comments that disagreed with the debunking nature of the main comments, and instead resorted to more xenophobic discourse. Thus, OPPOSING dialogic replies aligned with xenophobic values, and DISMISSING replies aligned with xenophobic and conspiratorial values. A desire to educate the audience was reflected in ADJUSTING replies, and RALLYING replies were a mixture of educating the audience or just calling out the YouTuber for spreading false information. DEFERRING replies were also a mixture of either xenophobic and skeptical values. In all, the replies to Anti-Conspiratorial comments featured more disagreement and xenophobic discourse.

Implications of findings and future directions

The results of this study have shown how affiliation is an important strategy for persuading others to align with the sets of social values proposed in YouTube discourse. The communing affiliation analysis conducted on the video transcripts showed which affiliation strategies were more frequently used in order to position audiences to align with these values. These strategies include addressing a community, emphasizing particular social bonds, and confining a social bond to a limited set of options. The dialogic affiliation analysis conducted on the comments of the videos, provided insight into how values are interactively negotiated. This analysis revealed how the particular social bonds propagated by YouTubers are not always directly affiliated with, and instead may be challenged or modified in the comment feed in order to suit the agendas of particular commenters, including rejecting the bonds proposed in the video entirely. At a macro-level, the results of this study illustrate how affiliation is an important strategy in terms of media logic and the mediatization of societal threats. On social media as with other forms of mass media, individuals and organizations adapt their communication to appeal to their audiences and the conventions of the media platform used. Affiliation is one such strategy for achieving these goals. By understanding how to linguistically identify affiliation strategies, this complements the valuable research already undertaken regarding the impact of societal threats mediatized online and how they can be counteracted.

To reflect on the overall significance of how this paper has engaged with current literature on white supremacist and conspiratorial discourse, and societal threats more broadly, it has achieved this in several ways. Firstly, the SFL method this paper outlines provides a way of delving deeper into the social values of conspiratorial communities identified by computational social science studies (such as Shahsavari et al., 2020) by highlighting the affiliation strategies used to make these social values prominent. Therefore, this paper can be of value to quantitative researchers wanting to understand the affiliative strategies of the most commonly identified social values in their datasets, or to qualitative researchers wanting to add another dimension of coding to their data by using linguistic terminology to articulate how communities are addressed and how social values are rejected or rallied around. Additionally, the results of this study relate to previous studies on the mediatization of societal threats (Krzyzanowski et al., 2018) by highlighting the power of rhetoric in "othering" certain groups in order to gain popularity and emphasizing how "the politics of fear" (Wodak, 2015) works at a discourse semantic level. Therefore, the results of this study engage with previous valuable research into the mediatization of societal threats but include the added dimension of affiliation in order to emphasize how social values are bonded around.

The methodology and results of this research are also applicable to a range of different case studies and applications. By being able to linguistically identify the different social values and affiliation strategies used in discourse, this means tailored responses to the issues of information disorder and hate speech can be developed, that do not attempt to homogenize the multiple reasons why people engage in such hateful behavior (Inwood & Zappavigna, forthcoming). These tailored responses would involve creating a linguistic profile for a specific community, outlining the social values and affiliative strategies particular to that community, and then developing strategies that can counteract this hateful discourse. These strategies need the input of both researchers and people who have lived experience in the communities studied in order to develop solutions. As Mahl et al (2022, p. 18) highlight, "national, cultural, and socio-political contexts" need to be taken into account when studying conspiracy theories and extremist discourse, meaning that "comparative studies across topics" also need to be developed if broader claims about conspiratorial communities are to be made. Thus, this study is one small contribution to numerous contributions that have been and need to be developed in order to counteract issues of information disorder and hate speech.

SFL approaches to studying white supremacy and extremist communication can also be useful in designing educational materials so that students can linguistically identify the language used by white supremacists and extremists and prevent themselves from becoming radicalized, as discussed by Szenes (2021). Understanding the importance of evaluative language and stance in white supremacist and conspiratorial discourse is an increased area of focus by researchers working across a range of discourse analysis perspectives (Demata, Zorzi, & Zottola, forthcoming; Szenes, 2021). So, this increased interest shows a need to further delineate hateful communities according to these linguistic strategies and collaboratively design materials that educate a diverse range of populations. In this sense, methods in SFL intersect with key issues raised in communication and media literacy studies, that highlight the complexity in effectively communicating the multi-layered issues at hand and translating academic results to varied audiences.

There are several ways in which this study can be expanded. At a technical level, the methodology used can be refined to identify patterns more closely in language and the relationship between affiliation strategies and specific social bonds. In terms of research impact, more collaboration could occur with linguistic and media disciplines to make the findings of this study more accessible for a broader audience. Additionally, this paper has just focused on one case study for analysis due to the time-consuming nature of manual discourse analysis, so in the future if more researchers adopt this methodology, further insights can be revealed regarding how affiliation strategies function across different case studies that utilize for example, different social media platforms or languages. Overall, this study has aimed to show the relevance of an SFL approach in developing critical ways to combat dangerous discourse, that intersects with key issues identified in media and communication studies.

Disclosure statement

The data that support the findings of this study are available from the corresponding author, Olivia Inwood, upon reasonable request.

Funding

Olivia Inwood receives an Australian Government Research Training Program Scholarship and additional funding support from the Commonwealth of Australia.

ORCID

Olivia Inwood http://orcid.org/0000-0001-6678-888X
Michele Zappavigna http://orcid.org/0000-0003-4004-9602

References

Allington, D., Buarque, B. L., & Barker Flores, D. (2021). Antisemitic conspiracy fantasy in the age of digital media: Three 'conspiracy theorists' and their YouTube audiences. *Language and Literature: International Journal of Stylistics*, 30(1), 78–102. doi:10.1177/0963947020971997
Altheide, D. L., & Snow, R. P. (1979). *Media logic*. Beverly Hills, California: Sage.
Anthony, L. A. (2014). Computer software. Tokyo, Japan: Waseda University.
Asakitikpi, A. O., & Gadzikwa, J. (2020). A critical discourse analysis of online Youtube news coverage of South African discourses on Xenophobia in democratic South Africa. *Politikon*, 47(4), 479–493. doi:10.1080/02589346.2020.1840022
Cassam, Quassim(2019). *Conspiracy Theories*. Cambridge: Polity
Couldry, N., & Hepp, A. (2013). Conceptualising mediatization: Contexts, traditions, arguments. *Communication Theory*, 23(3), 191–202. doi:10.1111/comt.12019
Culloty, E. (2020). Conspiracy and the epistemological challenges of mediatized conflict. In S. Maltby, B. O'Loughlin, K. Parry, & L. Roselle (Eds.), *Spaces of war, war of spaces* (pp. 83–102). New York, NY: Bloomsbury, .
Daniels, J. (2009). *Cyber racism: White supremacy online and the new attack on civil rights*. Maryland, MA: Rowman & Littlefield Publishers.

Demata, M., Zorzi, V., & Zottola, A. (forthcoming). Critical inquiries into the language of anti-science, post-trutherism, mis/disinformation and alternative media. In M. Demata, V. Zorzi, & A. Zottola (Eds.), *Conspiracy theory discourses*. Amsterdam, The Netherlands: John Benjamins ix–x .

Farkas, J., Schou, J., & Neumayer, C. (2018). Platformed antagonism: Racist discourses on fake Muslim Facebook pages. *Critical Discourse Studies, 15*(5), 463–480. doi:10.1080/17405904.2018.1450276

Finlayson, A. (2020). YouTube and political ideologies: Technology, populism and rhetorical form. *Political Studies*. doi:10.1177/0032321720934630

Fong, A., Roozenbeek, J., Goldwert, D., Rathje, S., & van der Linden, S. (2021). The language of conspiracy: A psychological analysis of speech used by conspiracy theorists and their followers on Twitter. *Group Processes & Intergroup Relations, 24*(4), 606–623. doi:10.1177/1368430220987596

Fuchs, C. (2018). "Dear Mr. Neo-Nazi, can you please give me your informed consent so that i can quote your fascist Tweet?": Questions of social media research ethics in online ideology critique. In G. Meikle (Ed.), *The Routledge companion to media and activism* (pp.385–394). Abington, Oxfordshire: Routledge .

Gillborn, D. (2006). Rethinking white supremacy: Who counts in 'WhiteWorld.' *Ethnicities, 6* (3), 318–340. doi:10.1177/1468796806068323

Halliday, M. A. K. (1978). *Language as social semiotic: The social interpretation of language and meaning*. London, United Kingdom: Hodder Arnold.

Halliday, M. A. K. (2008). Working with meaning: Towards an appliable linguistics. In J. Webster (Ed.), *Meaning in context: Implementing intelligent applications of language studies* (pp.7–23). London, UK: Continuum .

Harju, A. (2016). Imagined community and affective alignment in Steve Jobs memorial tributes on YouTube. In S. Gardner & S. Alsop (Eds.), *Systemic functional linguistics in the digital age* (pp.62–80). Sheffield, United Kingdom: Equinox Publishing .

Hokka, J. (2021). PewDiePie, racism and Youtube's neoliberalist interpretation of freedom of speech. *Convergence: The International Journal of Research into New Media Technologies, 27* (1), 142–160. doi:10.1177/1354856520938602

Inwood, O., & Zappavigna, M. (2021). Ambient affiliation, misinformation and moral panic: Negotiating social bonds in a YouTube internet hoax. *Discourse & Communication 15* (3), 1750481321989838.

Inwood, O., & Zappavigna, M. (forthcoming). The ID2020 conspiracy theory in YouTube video comments during COVID-19: Bonding around religious, political, and technological discourses. In M. Demata, V. Zorzi, & A. Zottola (Eds.), *Conspiracy Theory discourses* (pp. 241–266). Amsterdam, The Netherlands: John Benjamins .

Knight, N. K. (2010). *Laughing our bonds off: Conversational humour in relation to affiliation*. (PhD Thesis). University of Sydney, Unpublished.

Konkes, C., & Lester, L. (2015). Incomplete Knowledge, Rumour and Truth Seeking. *Journalism Studies, 18*(7), 826–844. doi:10.1080/1461670X.2015.1089182

Kopytowska, M. (2021). Xenophobia, misogyny and rape culture: Targeting women in cyberspace. *Journal of Language Aggression and Conflict, 9*(1), 76–99. doi:10.1075/jlac.00054.kop

Krzyzanowski, M. (2018). Discursive shifts in ethno-nationalist politics: On politicization and mediatization of the "Refugee crisis" in Poland. *Journal of Immigrant & Refugee Studies, 16* (1–2), 76–96. doi:10.1080/15562948.2017.1317897

Krzyzanowski, M., Triandafyllidou, A., & Wodak, R. (2018). the mediatization and the politicization of the "Refugee crisis" in Europe. *Journal of Immigrant & Refugee Studies, 16* (1–2), 1–14. doi:10.1080/15562948.2017.1353189

Lecompte-Van Poucke, M. (2022). 'You got this!': A critical discourse analysis of toxic positivity as a discursive construct on Facebook. *Applied Corpus Linguistics, 2*(1), 100015. doi:10.1016/j.acorp.2022.100015

Levy, H. (2020). Grammars of contestation and pluralism: Paulo Freire's action in Brazil's periphery and the rise of right-wing discourse on YouTube. *International Communication Gazette, 82*(5), 474–489. doi:10.1177/1748048520943696

Lim, S. S. (2020). Manufacturing hate 4.0: Can media studies rise to the challenge? *Television & New Media, 21*(6), 602–607. doi:10.1177/1527476420918825

Mahl, D., Schäfer, M. S., & Zeng, J. (2022). Conspiracy theories in online environments: An interdisciplinary literature review and agenda for future research. *New Media & Society* OnlineFirst , 14614448221075759.

Makki, M., & Zappavigna, M. (2021). Out-grouping and ambient affiliation in Donald Trump's tweets about Iran: Exploring the role of negative evaluation in enacting solidarity. *Pragmatics 32* (1), 104–130 .

Martin, J. R., & White, P. R. R. (2005). *The Language of Evaluation: Appraisal in English*. New York,NY: Palgrave Macmillan.

Matamoros-Fernández, A. (2017). Platformed racism: The mediation and circulation of an Australian race-based controversy on Twitter, Facebook and YouTube. *Information, Communication & Society, 20*(6), 930–946. doi:10.1080/1369118X.2017.1293130

Miller, D. T. (2021). Characterizing Qanon: Analysis of YouTube comments presents new conclusions about a popular conservative conspiracy. *First Monday*. doi:10.5210/fm.v26i2.10168

Murthy, D., & Sharma, S. (2019). Visualizing YouTube's comment space: Online hostility as a networked phenomena. *New Media & Society, 21*(1), 191–213. doi:10.1177/1461444818792393

Panizo-LLedot, A., Torregrosa, J., Bello-Orgaz, G., Thorburn, J., & Camacho, D. (2019). Describing Alt-Right Communities and Their Discourse on Twitter During the 2018 US Mid-term Elections Cherifi, H, Gaito, S, Mendes, J F. F., Moro, E, Rocha, L. M. In *International Conference on Complex Networks and Their Applications* (pp. 427–439). Cham: Springer.

Paolillo, J. C. (2018). The flat earth phenomenon on YouTube. *First Monday, 23*(12). doi:10.5210/fm.v23i12.8251

Rieder, B. (2015). *YouTube data tools (Version 1.11)*. Retrieved from https://tools.digitalmethods.net/netvizz/youtube/

Röchert, D., Neubaum, G., Ross, B., & Stieglitz, S. (2022). Caught in a networked collusion? Homogeneity in conspiracy-related discussion networks on YouTube. *Information Systems, 103*, 101866. doi:10.1016/j.is.2021.101866

Shahsavari, S., Holur, P., Wang, T., Tangherlini, T. R., & Roychowdhury, V. (2020). Conspiracy in the time of Corona: Automatic detection of emerging COVID-19 conspiracy theories in social media and the news. *Journal of Computational Social Science, 3*(2), 279–317. doi:10.1007/s42001-020-00086-5

Starbird, K., Arif, A., & Wilson, T. (2019). Disinformation as collaborative work: Surfacing the participatory nature of strategic information operations. *Proceedings of the ACM on Human-Computer Interaction, 3*(CSCW), 1–26. doi:10.1145/3359229

Supriadi, N. P., Gunawan, W., & Muniroh, R. D. D. A. (2020). Bullies' attitudes on Twitter: A forensic linguistics analysis of cyberbullying (Systemic functional linguistics approach). *Passage, 8*(2), 111–124.

Szenes, E. (2021). Neo-Nazi environmentalism: The linguistic construction of ecofascism in a Nordic resistance movement manifesto. *Journal for Deradicalization* Summer , (27), 146–192.

Thelwall, M., Sud, P., & Vis, F. (2012). Commenting on YouTube videos: From Guatemalan rock to el big bang. *Journal of the American Society for Information Science and Technology, 63*(3), 616–629. doi:10.1002/asi.21679

Wodak, R. (2015). *The politics of fear: What right-wing populist discourses mean.* Thousand Oaks, CA: Sage.

Wright, M. (2019). YouTube comment suite v1.4.2. Github. https://github.com/mattwright324/youtube-comment-suite

Zappavigna, M. (2011). Ambient affiliation: A linguistic perspective on Twitter. *New Media & Society, 13*(5), 788–806. doi:10.1177/1461444810385097

Zappavigna, M. (2018). *Searchable talk and social media metadiscourse.* London, UK: Bloomsbury Publishing.

Zappavigna, M. (2021). Ambient affiliation in comments on YouTube videos: Communing around values about ASMR. 外国语, *44*(1), 21–40.

Zappavigna, M., & Martin, J. R. (2018). # Communing affiliation: Social tagging as a resource for aligning around values in social media. *Discourse, Context & Media, 22,* 4–12. doi:10.1016/j.dcm.2017.08.001

🔓 OPEN ACCESS

Internet regulation and crisis-related resilience: From Covid-19 to existential risks

Gregory Asmolov

ABSTRACT
A broad literature on Internet regulation relies on imaginaries of the Internet as a socio-political technology. Deep mediatization of everyday life, however, increases the role of the Internet as a critical system for crisis response and mitigating global catastrophic risks. This article offers a theoretical contribution to exploring the role of regulation in crises through critical engagement with the concept of mediatization. The article addresses the question of what is "the meaning of Internet regulation in crisis situations and how it may diminish capacity to address future emergencies?" It stresses that understanding the consequences of mediatization in the context of future crises requires an exploration of Internet regulation from the mediational perspective and of the concept of generativity. Relying on an analysis of the role of digital platforms in Russia during the Covid-19 pandemic, the article illustrates how different forms of regulation limit resilience by restricting the generative potential of innovations that offer new forms of response to emerging threats. It highlights how the limitation of political freedoms in specific countries and the degree of global catastrophic risk are interrelated.

Introduction: internet regulation and crisis situations

The topic of Internet regulation has been addressed by a broad interdisciplinary literature. The analysis often goes beyond a focus on blocking specific types of content, filtering and censorship. Continuous mapping of new generations of Internet control (Deibert & Rohozinski, 2010) has identified more complicated regulative measures that are constantly evolving. On a national level, we see more efforts to implement new forms of Internet sovereignization that seek to allow state actors a scale and type of control over cyberspace equal to the scale and type of their control over physical space (Mueller, 2017). These efforts include not only legal measures, but also practices that seek to construct a "power vertical" in digital space (Gunitsky, 2015). Scholars are paying an increasing attention to the impact of regulating digital infrastructure on free expression and to new forms of state-sponsored algorithmic control not only

---

This is an Open Access article distributed under the terms of the Creative Commons Attribution License (http://creativecommons.org/licenses/by/4.0/), which permits unrestricted use, distribution, and reproduction in any medium, provided the original work is properly cited.

in authoritarian (Sivetc, 2021; Wijermars, 2021) but also in democratic countries (Freedom House, 2021, online).

An understanding of Internet regulation relies on understanding of different Internet imaginaries (Mansell, 2012). Debates around the tension between Internet regulation and Internet freedom rely on approaching the Internet as a liberation technology (Diamond & Plattner, 2010). Accordingly, regulation is approached as a limitation of political freedoms. Scholars who rely on approaches highlighting the roles of the Internet in economic production (Benkler, 2006) emphasize the socio-economic risks of Internet regulation. This study, however, stresses the need for an analysis of Internet regulation that relies on an understanding of the role of the Internet, beyond the socio-political and economic context. For this purpose, it explores the role of Internet regulation in crisis situations. Therefore, this article addresses the question: what are the potential consequences of Internet regulation in crisis situations for resilience, and how may it diminish the capacity to address "the next catastrophe" (Perrow, 2011)?

Exploring Internet regulation requires an analytical distinction between the concepts of risk and of crisis, as well as a highlighting of the link between these two concepts. The roles of digital platforms are accordingly distinguished between those of risk management and of crisis response. The first should help to prevent crisis by various digital means, e.g., the monitoring of potential trends that may lead to a crisis, and early warning, as well as the preparation of digital infrastructure that enables response that should mitigate the threat (Rogers & Pearce, 2016). The second is the role of platforms in various aspects of crisis response, including crisis mapping and resource mobilization to address the crisis (Alexander, 2014; Palen & Liu, 2007).

Different models offer frameworks that enable us to follow the transition from risk to crisis (Fink, 2002; Gonzalez-Herrero & Pratt, 1996), which can also be seen as a transition from everyday life in the shadow of potential crisis (Beck, 2006) to crisis-related social systems (Barton, 1969). On the one hand, the transformation of risk into crisis "can be seen as failures in risk management" (Sellnow & Sellnow, 2010, p. 116). On the other hand, a crisis starts a new cycle of post-crisis risk management. In this light, a crisis can be considered as an opportunity to examine the relationship between digital innovation and regulation in the context of a threat. However, this type of analysis also offers the potential value of considering the impact of regulation on addressing future crises presented through various forms of risk communication.

The state of risk and the state of crisis are linked by the notion of resilience. According to Tierney (2014), resilience involves "pre-existing, planned, and naturally emerging activities that make societies and communities better able to cope, adapt, and sustain themselves when disasters occur, and also to develop ways of recovering following such events" (2014, p. 5). In this light, she defines risk as "the possibility of serious disturbance to the integrity of a system" (p. 5). Here we may distinguish between risk and resilience. The notion of risk concerns what may potentially go wrong, explores its likelihood and consequences. Resilience is a feature of the system potentially facing the risk. The importance of resilience highlights the need to identify the factors and policies that may contribute to either increasing or restricting resilience. The purpose of this article is therefore to offer a conceptualization of the role of digital platforms in the development of resilience, and accordingly of the policies that may limit resilience and increase social fragility following the transformation from risk into crisis.

The notion of resilience is particularly important in the context of the discussion regarding existential risks including the risks that associated with pandemics and climate change. Existential risks are a specific type of global catastrophic risks, where the damage is not only global but also terminal and permanent (Bostrom, 2002). The impact of Internet regulation on the development of resilience may be further seen as significant in the context of the literature on global catastrophic and existential risks (Bostrom & Ćirković, 2008). While a rich literature explores the political implications of Internet regulation, the link between Internet regulation and the capacity to mitigate global catastrophic and existential risks remains unexplored. Here the question concerns whether the contribution of digital platforms to resilience may diminish the catastrophic risks, and what are the condition that may allow the transformation of potential catastrophes into non-existential crises.

The classification of global catastrophic risks by Avin et al. (2018) suggests that an analysis of these risks should be considered through three vectors: "The critical system whose safety boundaries are breached by a potential threat"; "the mechanisms by which this threat might spread globally" and "the manner in which we might fail to prevent or to mitigate both" (Avin et al., 2018, p. 21). Based on this framework, one may argue that global information networks have a triple significance: they are critical to supporting our lives, they can be used to spread different threats (as in the case of the "infodemic"), and they can be an important mechanism for responding to crises. The last point allows us to contextualize resilience as linked to mitigation, whereas the Internet can be considered as a critical system for the prevention and mitigation of global catastrophic risks.

In order to address the research question, the next section offers a theoretical framework that enables us to explore the potential impact of Internet regulation on the development of resilience. Based on critical reflection regarding the role of Internet regulation through the lens of mediatization, this section suggests that the vital role of the Internet in addressing global catastrophic risks can be seen from a mediational perspective. This perspective enables us to go beyond a focus on the construction of the risk and of the crisis, and to explore the generativity of digital platforms as a major factor in shaping new forms of user-crisis relationship. In such a case, regulation concerns not only the crisis as an object, but also users as subjects, as well as the role of digital tools that offer new forms of users-crisis mediated relationships.

Relying on this theoretical framework, the following section suggests a methodological framework that allows us to consider the impact of Internet regulation on resilience in the face of crisis. This framework allows us to focus on an analysis of the impact of regulation on three elements of the mediational triangle: crisis as object, the users of digital platforms as subjects, and the role of digital tools as mediators of subject-object relationships. This framework offers an empirical opportunity for exploring the generativity of digital platforms in the construction of user-crisis relationships through mapping the structure of crisis-related activity systems. It highlights the generativity of platforms in crisis situations as the core factor, when resilience cannot be sustained, if any elements of the triangle are constrained by regulative policies.

The role of generativity in the context of digitally-mediated relationship between users and crisis is addressed here through empirical analysis of Internet regulation in response to the Covid-19 pandemic. This analysis of the role of digital platforms in Covid-19 response in Russia allows us to identify the regulative efforts applied to each element of the triangle, and accordingly to the entire system of crisis-related activity. The discussion shows how regulation limits not only crisis response, but also post-crisis transformation that fails to offer a new level of resilience resulting from efforts of regulation.

Internet regulation in crises: from mediatization to a mediational perspective

Conceptualization of the role of Internet regulation in crisis response is essential in order to explore the link between regulation and the development of resilience. Many approaches to regulation may focus analytical attention mainly on the communicative processes and relations of power involved in the construction of risks and crises. For instance, according to Entman (1993), the framing of a crisis evokes several significant questions, including who is responsible for the crisis and how the crisis should be addressed. In this light, exogenous threats (as in the cases of either natural disaster or armed conflict) can also lead to a chain effect and to a destabilization of the internal socio-political situation in the context of the relationship between authorities and citizens (Pelling & Dill, 2006).

A variety of digital tools play an active role in the symbolic construction of a crisis, including its framing of the attribution of responsibility (Coombs & Holladay, 2004). Moreover, various types of framing may lead to various forms of social mobilization, and to channeling the attention of the public toward either direct response or criticism of the authorities. In some cases, what starts as a crisis-related mobilization can rapidly shift into protests against the institutions responsible for crisis management. At the same time, some framings may mitigate the risk to the authorities from independent mobilization. In this light, Internet regulation can be considered as a policy seeking to take control over the symbolic construction of the crisis and diminish the political risks related to crisis situations.

A more nuanced understanding of the role of Internet regulation in crisis response can be identified, based on the application of the mediatization concept. Esser and Matthes define mediatization as the increasing "intrusion of media logic" into various fields (2013, p. 177). Mediatization changes the way disasters are experienced by a broad audience (Cottle, 2006). It also offers new forms of control over crisis. The notion of *arrested war* (Hoskins & O'Loughlin, 2015) suggests that the chaos of user-generated content has been harnessed by institutional actors who developed capacity to control the ways in which media logic shapes the construction of crises.

A new stage in the development of mediatization theory suggests, however, that we need to move beyond a focus on the role of media logic in the construction of crises. The notion of *deep mediatization* highlights how new media technologies transform the nature of crisis situations as a part of everyday life. According to Couldry and Hepp, "Deep mediatization is an advanced stage of the process in which all elements of our social world are intricately related to digital media and their underlying infrastructures" (2017, p. 7). In such a case, crisis situations cannot be separated from platforms and their algorithms. A discussion of regulation, therefore, should increase the scope of the factors to be considered beyond symbolic construction to include the role of platforms.

Hepp also highlights the fact that that deep mediatization involves physical activity and collaboration, while "the separation between communicative action and physical action becomes blurred" (Hepp, 2020, p. 11). Accordingly, relying on the concept of deep mediatization suggests that Internet regulation involves regulating a broad range of individual and collective actions. However, the key challenge of applying deep mediatization as a framework for regulation analysis is the broad nature of the concept, which does not allow us to identify the specific consequences of mediatization in a crisis context and to develop a consistent methodological framework.

While Internet regulation in terms of a traditional mediatization concerns taking control of the role of media logic in shaping the nature of an event, Internet regulation in a time of deep mediatization is related to regulating digital infrastructure in a way that increasingly expands control over everyday life. Hepp's argument regarding the role of mediatization in physical action reminds us, however, of a different analytical tradition that can offer a framework for the analysis of Internet regulation in the context of crisis and its impact on resilience. This involves the concept of mediated activity initially developed in the context of cultural-historical activity theory (CHAT).

The role of mediation was conceptualized by Vygotsky as a triangle with three key elements: subject, tools, and objects (Vygotsky, 1978). The subject in this case is the individual person, while the object of the subject's activity is the environment. The tools link subject and object, and this linkage is conceptualized as a mediation of activity. According to Kaptelinin, "technology is considered as mediating means that affects, and even shapes, the structure, functioning and development of human mind and action" (Kaptelinin, 2014, p. 203). Kaptelinin and Nardi (2006, p. 32) consider activity "as the basic unit of analysis providing a way to understand both subjects and objects." Engeström developed an analytical framework for the analysis of collective activity, defining activity systems as "systems of collaborative human practice" (Engeström, 1988, p. 30). Digital mediation is therefore seen in the context of activity systems that offer a system of relationships between subjects (users) and their environment (objects).

In this light, digital tools offered by the Internet play an essential role in the relationship between users and crises, as well as between users and other actors (including institutions) in the context of a crisis. This relationship relies on three elements: the definition of a crisis as a potential object of activity, the attribution of responsibility for a crisis in the context of a relationship with other actors, and the mediated relationships with the crisis. In this sense, mediation has a double role, whereby a symbolic mediation of meanings is associated with the mediation of activities in response to the crisis (and to the actors identified as responsible). The role of Internet regulation is therefore concerned mostly with how control over digital platforms may shape relationships between users and crisis.

In response to the Covid-19 pandemic, Ferholt et al. (2020) suggest the notion of "humanity's leading activity" as "the activity whose development accounts for the most important changes in humanity's response to current and forthcoming crises" including "a struggle for survival and against extinction of the species" (p. 96). A focus on "the increasingly digitalized nature of human activity encompassing humans, algorithms, augmented intelligence, and other digital technologies" (Karanasios, Nardi, Spinuzzi, & Malaurent, 2021, pp. 234–235) reminds us of the approach of deep mediatization scholars. Here, as a compromise between two approaches, we may talk about a *deep mediatization of activity*.

Karanasios et al. (2021) link this transformation of the nature of human activity to the generative capacity of digital platforms. The notion of generativity has been introduced by Zittrian as "a capacity to produce unanticipated change through unfiltered contributions from broad and varied audiences" (Zittrain, 2008, p. 70). The generative capacity of the Internet allows "technology to produce new activities and outputs and to structure behavior beyond original creators' intentions" (Karanasios et al., 2021, p. 245). Generativity as the capacity to introduce unanticipated forms of subject-object relationships relying on digital mediation in crisis situations can be considered an essential element for the development of resilience. A generative system not only creates new meanings, but also mediates new forms of relationship between subject and surrounding environment. In other words, generative systems formulate new goals on the level of meaning, and offer new mechanisms for accomplishing these on the level of activity. Accordingly, Internet regulation can be considered as a set of policies that may limit the generative capacity of digital platforms and diminish resilience in the face of future crises.

A framework that relies on a concept of *generativity* (Zittrain, 2008) allows us to offer an argument for how Internet regulation may diminish our capacity to address global catastrophic risks (Bostrom, 2002). The notion of *preadaptation* (Cuénot, 1914), although it was introduced before the era of the Internet, offers a fruitful contribution to this framework. It describes systems with resources that may seem to be redundant, but can play a key role in survival in the face of new risks. Such a framework argues that the Internet enhances processes that increase socio-cultural diversity, thereby raising both its preadaptive potential and its sensitivity to change. In this sense, the Internet can be considered as a system that encourages the development of variability and preadaptation, and a resource that allows a system to react to crises (Asmolov, 1998).

In that light, more attention needs to be dedicated to considering Internet regulation in terms of the potential of the Internet to offer crisis-related innovation and crisis-related entrepreneurship (Nambisan, 2017), and to addressing institutional voids (Khanna & Palepu, 2010), that may potentially emerge in the context of future crises. In this sense, Internet regulation may diminish the capacity of digital innovation to offer new forms of subject-object relationships in the face of future crises. An analysis of Internet regulation requires us to rely on a methodological framework that draws on a mediational perspective and focuses on activity systems as the primary units of analysis. This framework should help us to examine how Internet regulation may influence the development of new potential forms of user-crisis relationships and on the generative transformation of human activity in the face of crisis in a deeply mediatized environment.

Methodology: internet regulation and the structure of crisis-related activity systems

The purpose of this methodological framework is to offer a systematic way of assessing the impact of Internet regulation on the capacity of digital platforms to introduce new forms of activity in response to a crisis. This analysis concerns the impact of regulation on the generativity of platforms, and accordingly on the capacity of digital innovation to mitigate future risks and to increase the scale of social resilience. The mediational perspective suggests a focus on activity as the major level of analysis. Accordingly, the role of digital mediation is addressed in the context of relationships between subjects and objects, for example in the case of relationships between users and crisis situations, as well as of subject-to-subject relationships such as those between individual and institutional actors in the context of a crisis. More specifically, the framework suggests the need to examine the impact of internet regulation on the structure of crisis-related activity systems:

(I) The focus on the ***object*** suggests an exploration of defining the object of activity that requires the mobilization of users' resources and the development of new forms of activity. Different forms of regulation may potentially restrict the freedom to define a crisis, and limit the capacity of other actors to introduce their own definitions of the crisis as a potential object of activity.

(II) The focus on the ***subject*** proposes an exploration of how regulation constructs and restricts the role of digital users in the context of crisis situations, how the role of users is viewed by institutional actors, and specifically how they are approached either as partners for collaboration or as objects of control.

(III) The key object of regulation is the emergence of new forms of relationship between people and crisis, relying on the restriction of generativity. The focus on digital platforms as ***mediating tools*** suggests an exploration of how the regulation of platforms and innovation shapes the nature of user-crisis relationships and limits/enables new forms of activity in relation to a crisis. It also allows us to address the degree of generativity based on an analysis of the extent to which existing tools support rapid development of new forms of subject-object relationships in the context of a crisis.

Through its focus on the impact of regulation on the construction of crisis-related objects, the construction of subjects, and the role of digital tools in subject-object relationships, this methodological framework allows us to explore the role of digital platforms in identifying risk, in attributing responsibility for risk, and in forms of activity in relation to the risk. In this way, new forms of user-crisis relationships rely both on the symbolic construction of crisis and on the development of new forms of digital mediation in order to mobilize resources to address the crisis. The latter suggests digital sourcing in the context of a crisis as of particular interest for research that explores the role of regulation.

A generativity of activity means a constant emergence of new forms of resource mobilization to address crisis-related goals. On the collective level, a generative system of activity offers new tools for the formation of dynamic activity networks around a broad spectrum of goals. One such practice is crowdsourcing, a set of technologies that allows the mobilization of individuals' resources via a network in the name of goals arising within a generative system. That suggests exploring to what extent new forms of Internet regulation either restrict or enable new forms of mobilization of resources.

The Covid-19 pandemic offers an empirical opportunity to address the role of Internet regulation in the development of resilience. Due to the global nature of the crisis, Covid-19 can be seen as a type of emergency with some features that have been described in the literature on global catastrophic risks. Therefore, exploring the impact of Internet regulation of Covid-19 is fruitful for a discussion of the role of digital platforms in the mitigation of global catastrophic risks. In addition, Covid-19 offers opportunities for comparative analysis of the role of digital platforms and regulation, since the same crisis has been addressed in many countries.

This article explores the role of digital platforms and regulation in the response to Covid-19 in Russia. There are several reasons why Russia was selected as a case in order to discuss the advantages of the theoretical argument of this article regarding the impact of Internet regulation on generativity and resilience in the face of existential risk, and to illustrate the application of a methodological framework that derives from this argument. First, the Internet and digital innovation in Russia are to be seen under the increasing pressure of different forms of regulation. Over the last ten years, the Russian authorities have substantially increased their control over the Internet (Klyueva, 2016). The Russian parliament has approved numerous laws that seek to impose new forms of Internet regulation, including the so-called "Internet Sovereignty Bill" introduced in 2019. This regulation has been manifested also through a diversity of economic and political measures, including digital innovation by state actors that seeks to reduce independent forms of mobilization and to develop advanced surveillance capabilities (Ermoshina, Loveluck, & Musiani, 2021).

Second, over the last ten years, Russia has experienced numerous emergencies and disasters that led to a broad range of crisis-related digital innovations (Samoilenko, 2016). Rapid change in the regulatory environment in Russia allows us to conduct a comparative analysis of the role of platforms in different regulative contexts within the same country. Therefore, the Russian case offers an empirical opportunity to examine how the role of digital platforms in emergency response has changed in the context of increasing state-sponsored Internet regulation. The Russian wildfires of 2010 can be considered as the first major disaster to take place in the context of an active proliferation of social networks and social media. It also took place in the context of the global development of a crisis-mapping movement relying on the availability of satellite imagery, open-source maps and new crowdsourcing tools (Meier, 2015).

The Russian state, lagging behind in the area of crisis mobilization, has embarked since the 2010 crisis on the development of new technologies. These were intended to return control of crisis-related mobilization resources to the state and to minimize the political risks associated with the independent crisis-related activity of users. New forms of "vertical crowdsourcing" (Asmolov, 2015) can be considered as forms of state-sponsored innovation, the essence of which is an attempt to integrate the horizontal mobilization of the volunteer community into Russia's vertical power structures. Vertical crowdsourcing can also be seen as a new form of control through regulation of user-crisis relationships. In this light, given the particular concern of the Russian authorities regarding the role of digital platforms in crisis situations, the increasing scope of Internet regulation and the record of crisis-related innovation, a focus on the response to Covid-19 in Russia presents an opportunity to explore the impact of regulation on digitally mediated crisis response.

This analysis has relied on collection of data about Covid-related digital projects developed between January 2020 and September 2020. The analysis identified 14 digital initiatives, including state-sponsored and independent projects. That included crowdsourcing projects that offered various forms of mobilization concerning Covid-19, crisis mapping projects and Covid-related tracking apps. Some projects relied on several tools, including Telegram channels and chatbots. The data collection has addressed two aspects. First, the project's structure and its modus of operations to analyze how these tools mediated user-crisis relationships. Second is the coverage of the projects in Russian media. An additional data set included statements by Russian officials regarding the role of digital platforms in crisis response. Lastly, a series of events with the founders of crisis-related projects was organized with a partner in Russia. The events allowed us to collect data concerning the obstacles for the operation of independent projects. The data collected was analyzed on the basis of a thematic framework (Boyatzis, 1998) developed by relying on the elements of a mediational triangle: regulation of subject, regulation of object, and regulation of mediating digital tools. NVivo was used to conduct thematic analysis of the data relying on the coding framework.

Generativity and crisis response in Russia: the case of Covid-19

This section explores the link between Internet regulation and crisis response in Russia. The analysis considers whether, and if so how, increasing Internet regulation limits the crisis-related resilience of a society. The section is divided into three parts based on the methodological framework: regulation of objects; regulation of subjects; regulation and mediating tools.

Regulation of objects

Crisis communication literature traditionally highlights how the construction of a crisis is a crucial factor in the attribution of blame (Coombs & Holladay, 2004). This is related not only to human-made crises, but also to natural disasters where the authorities are held accountable for the efficiency of their engagement. Governments in almost all countries have faced criticism and scrutiny regarding their policies and crisis management skills in response to Covid-19. A wave of protests and calls for resignations of political leaders due to their poor managements of the crisis have been seen in many countries.

In this light, it is important for a government to show that a crisis is under full control. This type of effort has been seen during all crises in Russia since the wildfires in 2010 (Bertrand, 2012). An issue of particular sensitivity is the number of casualties, since this offers a metric for the scale of the crisis and the efficiency of state efforts. Attempts to manipulate official statistics based on these numbers have also been seen in the recent history of Russian crisis response. The framework of this study highlights, however, that the construction of the object needs to be seen in the context of an activity system. On the one hand, if the construction of a crisis suggests the absence of a proper response from state authorities, this may suggest the need for activities in relation to institutional actors to hold them accountable and force them to act properly (e.g., protests). On the other hand, the construction of the object is associated with the nature of activities of citizens in relation to the crisis. A construction of the crisis as an object under the full control of institutional actors suggests that there is no need for independent activities in response to the crisis. However, if the crisis is constructed as an object that is out of control, then this offers more space for the emergence of independent crisis-related action.

In the case of Covid-19, we have seen how new legislation targeting so-called "fake news" is used to prohibit the proliferation of alternative interpretations of the crisis. In June 2020, Russia's Prosecutor General's office reported a spike in Covid-related "fakes" on the Internet, adding that actions were being taken "to restrict access to 180 Internet resources" (Agora International Human Rights Group, 2020, online). According to the Russian human rights group AGORA (2020, online), the criminalization of fake news "has become a convenient tool for reprisal against the authorities' critics." The concept of fake news became a crisis-management tool, allowing authorities to shift responsibility toward those spreading it. Russian authorities have blamed the EU and the US for distributing Covid-related fake news in order to destabilize the socio-political situation in Russia.

As a goal of social mobilization, this response to "fakes" essentially replaces the public response to a crisis or public scrutiny of the state's efficiency. Websites like *coronafake.ru* were launched by state-sponsored actors to engage the public in participatory identification of what is considered by state institutions to be fake. The concept of participatory propaganda (Asmolov, 2019) highlights how state actors engage users in order to produce and distribute content. This participation, however, is focused also on the identification of content that is considered "fake" because it contradicts the official position (for example, because it offers alternative data about the number of victims). The state-sponsored participation in identifying fakes can be considered as the creation of an alternative object of mobilization. It refocuses public attention away from the problem of the virus. The fake news argument can be also considered a social construction that helps to delegitimize independent sources of information.

In addition to the focus on fakes, state-sponsored media coverage of volunteering has been focused on the construction of narrow and restricted objects of mobilization, such as assistance to elderly people unable to purchase essentials due to Covid isolation, while excluding alternative objects of mobilization that may potentially expose the failure of institutional actors (e.g., related to support for medical staff). In this way, the state-sponsored channeling of participation could be viewed not only in relation to engagement with the crisis, but also as a construction of the crisis.

The major object of concern, however, is related to the discussion of subjects, the public and users as responsible for the crisis. Here the construction of object and subject are deeply interrelated, since the regulative efforts seem to transform people seen as a potential resource into people seen as a problem (e.g., due to refusal to be vaccinated or failure to obey isolation rules), which can be considered as an objectification of subjects and as a strategy for shifting the attribution of blame from institutional actors to the public.

Regulation of subjects

The major tension concerns whether the construction of a subject is associated with potential forms of activity or of passivity of the subject in the context of a crisis situation. This depends on whether the subject is potentially constructed as a resource/partner for mobilization that can be engaged by addressing the object, or is a part of the problem that needs to be solved in the context of the crisis, and accordingly an object in itself.

Various forms of digital surveillance construct the user as an object of control and a potential source of risk. Tracking apps have been introduced in many countries during Covid-19, however these applications vary depending on the degree of intrusion into the personal sphere. Covid-related monitoring has also relied on the existing structure of surveillance of a society. This relies on the consolidation of "surveillance systems whose existence dates back several years" (Musiani et al., 2021p. 175). For instance, the surveillance cameras with a face recognition function that were installed as a part of the "Safe City" program in Moscow were used to identify people who broke quarantine rules during lockdown. Another case of surveillance is presented by a Russian application known as "Social Monitoring" that was created to make sure Russian citizens complied with self-confinement. It tracked users via GPS and sent them notifications at random times demanding that they share a selfie to prove they were at home. The app, however, created multiple controversies after many people received fines as a result of glitches, although they were following quarantine rules.

The tension around the construction of a subject in the context of a crisis can also be seen in the context of hyperlocal networks. Here one could identify two competing models of the subject in the relationship between neighbors. On the one hand, a subject can be interpreted within a context of mutual aid as a first responder and immediate resource that can be mobilized to help. On the other hand, a subject can be considered a risk to the community that may potentially violate the rules and therefore need to be surveilled. COVIDarity (https://covidarnost.ru/), a digital initiative attempting to support the development of horizontal neighborhood mutual-aid groups, was launched in March 2020 by activist Alexandra Krylenkova. "In a situation where the state does not make decisions to act against the crisis, civil society should act," Krylenkova wrote on her Facebook page.[1] The goal of this project was to organize information about local mutual-aid communities. A COVIDarity group chat was created on Telegram, as well as a chat bot on Telegram designed to give users information about a local mutual-aid chat in their building or to help them create such a chat in their area.

According to Krylenkova, the construction of the subject on a hyperlocal level was associated with a preexisting experience of collaboration on that level that allowed the development of some degree of trust: "It worked where communities have already existed in homes, and had a previous experience of solving specific hyperlocal problems (e.g., parking issues). Where there were no existing communities, new communities were not created, despite many efforts that we invested in this" (online workshop, 2021).

At the same time, a state-sponsored system has tried to develop an alternative model for the construction of neighbors. Various tracking systems and online maps launched by state-sponsored media have supported forms of horizontal surveillance among neighbors. For example, maps showing addresses where a virus carrier had been discovered were created by the Mash project (*coronavirus.mash.ru*). Local city forums were also used for the persecution of the sick and their relatives by neighbors. In the eyes of the vigilantes, neighbors were not a subject of mutual aid, but an object of observation and a potential threat. According to Mikhail Klimarev,

---

[1] https://www.facebook.com/krylenkova/posts/3073652779419055.

a Russian Internet freedom activist, digital surveillance tends to "infantilizes citizens and suppress civic responsibility" (Musiani et al., 2021, p. 176). According to Moscow Mayor Sergei Sobyanin, Muscovites were reacting to their neighbors who violated the regime of self-isolation even more toughly than the police were.[2]

Trust seems to be a crucial factor for the construction of a subject in a crisis situation, as shown by this case of relationships within hyperlocal networks. While there is widespread evidence of "lack of mutual trust between citizens and the state" (Musiani et al., 2021, p. 176), the state has tried to solve this problem by enhancing the lack of trust among people and diverting mistrust away from institutional and toward individual actors. Additionally, the emphasis on distrust leads to digital vigilantism, resulting in the Internet's horizontal structures being used, in times of crisis, for mutual surveillance as opposed to mutual assistance. In this light, some of the regulation seems to limit opportunities for digitally mediated horizontal mobilization, while replacing objects of activity in a situation of crisis with subjects. The external threat (e.g., virus or fires) has been replaced for people as an object. This transformation of activity has been supported by digital vigilantism activities.

According to Johnston (1996), vigilantes can be considered as citizens who appoint themselves to enforce justice against other citizens without having the legal authority to do this. Some vigilantes are driven by the perception that the government is incapable of enforcing the law, while others emerge in the context of informal state-public partnerships. State-sponsored digital vigilantism has been seen as a form of participatory regulation and surveillance in an authoritarian environment (Loveluck, 2019). For instance, Russian authorities have launched multiple "cyber guard" projects that engage users in Internet regulation through the detection of so-called extremist content (Dauce et al., 2020). This engagement in hyperlocal surveillance continues the logic of participatory regulation. In such a situation, digital vigilantism replaces mutual aid as a dominant form of mobilization in a crisis context. Digital vigilantism can also be considered as a form of mobilization that weakens independent crisis-related activity systems, as well as citizen-driven activity systems that may challenge state actors.

An additional form of regulation of the subject can be seen in the facilitation of polarization within horizontal connections between individuals. The disconnective power of disinformation campaigns that aim to dissolve horizontal ties among people by increasing the impact of crisis-related social categorization has been noted previously in the context of the Russia-Ukraine war (Asmolov, 2018). This manifestation of disconnective power allows a state to construct users by setting particular aspects of the crisis as social markers in interpersonal communication. In the case of Covid-19, a shift of blame for the

---

[2] https://tass.ru/moskva/8,159,779.

crisis toward the irresponsibility of the public have sustained the phenomenon of online "unfriending." Polarization and continuous disconnection based on attitudes to vaccination can be seen as an effort to construct subjects in a way that reduces mutual trust and sabotages independent networked collaboration in response to the crisis.

Regulation of tools

As in many other countries, the Covid-19 crisis in Russia was followed by a wave of crisis-related innovation. This included the development both of independent digital projects and of projects sponsored and promoted by official state institutions. Some hackathons, as an online Covidhack event, took place to facilitate collaboration within the IT community to address the challenge (Musiani et al., 2021). A major focus of independent initiatives was the facilitation of mutual aid. This included not only the COVIDarity project described above, but also hyperlocal groups that had arisen on the basis of instant messengers and relied on Telegram chatbots. For instance, Russian political activist Yegor Zhukov launched a Telegram bot *@mutualhelp*, which allowed users either to ask for help or to volunteer.

The Russian liberal newspaper *Novaya Gazeta* created the Corona-Info Telegram bot *(@corona_tgbot)*, acting as an aggregator for volunteer initiatives to support the ecosystem that emerged from various mobilization tools. An independent project, Memedic (*Memedic.ru*), offered a transparent system for medical volunteering that allowed people to sign up for shifts in hospitals. The founder of the project explained the need for the system in terms of the inefficiency of official state-sponsored "Medical Volunteers" (online workshop, 2021). Some platforms were created in the Russian regions to support collaboration between local NGOs. For instance, in Perm a coalition of NGOs launched a neighborhood mutual-aid action, the *Sosediperm.ru* website, which facilitated dialogue between individual users and organizations in order to identify opportunities to provide help. An additional example of independent mobilization can be seen in the case of a community of "makers" that used 3-D printers to create personal protective equipment. The mobilization of such "makers" has become a global phenomenon. Dozens of regional groups of makers appeared on Telegram under a title *Makers vs. COVID*, where activists discuss the production process and coordinate the transfer of the items they have created to medical institutions.

The major feature of most of these independent projects was a high degree of generativity. The users could either create new tasks or/and identify a task for their mobilization. There was no need for a complicated process of registration, approval or confirmation in order to enable participation (though each project had some specific rules). Due to a transparent structure, people had more agency over their participation in crisis response. The projects were evolving fast in order to address new challenges, and engaged the community to support the technological development driven by new emerging challenges. Hyperlocal projects had the highest degree of generativity, since they were created to support horizontal mobilization of the resources of local communities around any type of goal based on the decentralized architecture of a platform. However, many of these projects faced substantial challenges in light of state regulation.

No matter how effective the mobilization tools, these cannot work unless a wide audience learns about them. Therefore, the role of media in proliferating information about these projects is crucial to their success. However, the media can also be a tool for demobilization. Russian state-sponsored media contributed to limiting the role of independent projects. A number of informal mutual-aid projects became the subjects of information attacks designed to challenge the legitimacy of independent mobilization tools. For example, an article in *Nezavisimaya Gazeta*, published under the heading "COVIDarity turned out to be an opposition project," emphasized that mutual-aid projects could help the Kremlin's political rivals gain political capital. A number of pro-government media platforms, argued that some of the independent projects operate for the sake of panic in society, while financial fraud might be hidden behind a screen of mutual aid.

At the same time, Russian media were managing an intensive PR campaign in order to promote state-sponsored volunteering portals that were used to mobilize the public to address Covid-19. The *Dobro.ru* portal (Portal of Goodness) became a central hub for the "We are Together" campaign launched by Russian authorities to mobilize volunteers in response to Coronavirus. The portal was a part of the Volunteers of Russia unified information system, supported by state agencies. The architecture of the *Dobro.ru* corresponds to the centralized principles of "vertical crowdsourcing" (Asmolov, 2015). A person who wants to become a volunteer is registered, fills out a questionnaire, and waits to be called upon to fight the crisis. Another volunteering project was launched by the Russia Today (RT) TV channel. RT's Mutual Aid Map (https://ddbm.rt.com/) allowed anyone to register themselves as a volunteer by indicating their place of residence, or to post a request for help. This map had a transparent structure, although it relied on a list of strict service rules and legal limitations. Data from April 2020 also showed a significant imbalance between a high number of volunteers (more than 2,000) and low number of applications for assistance (about 20).

To sum up, the Russian ecosystem of volunteering that has arisen around COVID-19 is characterized by a predominance of digital platforms with some relation to the state, and by the crowding out of independent projects. The active promotion of pro-state platforms can be also seen as regulation limiting decentralized, hyperlocal and generative tools, while giving preference to tools of vertical crowdsourcing that offer an opportunity to keep crisis-related mobilization of the public under strict control, and to limit the scope of public participation in crisis response. In this light, we may argue that state-sponsored digital platforms have played a dominant role in defining the relationship between the Russian public and Covid-19, and in regulating the mobilization of people's resources in relation to the crisis.

Discussion

The purpose of this article has been to explore the potential consequences of regulation for crisis response and the development of resilience in the face of future risks in a deeply mediatized environment. The integration of a mediation perspective and the notion of generativity offered an opportunity to present an argument regarding the impact of regulation. It suggested that we explore the impact of Internet regulation on the structure of crisis-related activity systems. This focus allows us to argue that the major contribution of generativity to the development of resilience can be seen in the role of platforms in the relationships between users and crisis situations, when different forms of state-sponsored regulation limit the potential of platforms to offer new forms of response to a crisis.

An analysis of the role of digital platforms in response to the Covid-19 pandemic in Russia has allowed us to illustrate this argument. On the one hand, we see various efforts by the regulator to keep the construction of the crisis under control. The regulation of an object can be associated with different forms of mobilization to address this object, and accordingly may limit the role of digital platforms in crisis-related mobilization. Moreover, we see the efforts of the state to replace the object by shifting attention from the crisis to other actors. The regulation of the subject has relied on variety of policies, starting with new legal restrictions, tracking apps and state-sponsored media narratives that aim to shift the balance of trust from mistrust of authorities to mistrust of the public, and online initiatives that support digital vigilantism. Finally, we see the tension between, on the one hand, independent, decentralized tools that offer a flexible structure for user-crisis relationships and enable a high degree of generativity, and, on the other hand, state-sponsored platforms that limit the scope of participation and follow the logic of vertical crowdsourcing.

Overall, this empirical discussion demonstrates how an integration of different forms of regulation restricts the generativity capacity of digital platforms to produce new forms of relationship to a crisis, including new forms of resources mobilization. It also weakens horizontal and hyperlocal networks that may potentially create alternative, decentralized systems of crisis-related mobilization beyond state control. The main victim of these regulative efforts is the resilience of society in the face of future crises, its capacity to offer rapid innovation and new forms of user-crisis relationships depending on the nature of the threat by relying on existing and new digital tools.

By drawing on the concept of generativity, this empirical analysis demonstrates the role of the Internet in an increasing variety of activities mediated by digital tools, specifically crowdsourcing and commons-based production practices, in response to Covid-19. The empirical case also highlights the value of new forms of digital mediation between users and their environments, as well as of the generative capacity of the Internet to produce new forms of activity, in the context of the emergence of global catastrophic risks. This includes the role of digital tools both, on the one hand, in detecting a crisis and constructing it as a potential object of activity and, on the other hand, in mobilizing resources to address the threat. The notion of preadaptation highlights how, as a generative environment, the Internet should be considered as a source of latent resources that may seem not to be necessary, but can potentially play a crucial role in the response to crises. Preexisting hyperlocal networks seem to be a particularly important resource of preadaptation, while these empirical insights suggest that it has been challenging to form new hyperlocal networks during this crisis.

The change in the role of digital platforms for crisis response in Russia offers an empirical illustration of the potential impact of Internet regulation on future crisis response. A range of regulatory measures, including traditional censorship, regulation of disinformation as defined by the state, indirect support for digital vigilantism, facilitation of disconnection within horizontal structures, and participatory forms of regulation through an orchestration of mobilization, can be seen as an effort to control subject-object relationships in the context of a crisis. Such control relies on a combination of using digital platforms to define the risk, attributing responsibility (either to external forces or to public), and offering a structure of activity systems that are fully integrated into the state framework for crisis response. The latter also includes a redirection of citizen mobilization away from independent channels toward either state-sponsored channels or/and "thin" forms participation (Zuckerman, 2014).

Although this discussion relies on the empirical case from Russia, the value of this framework can be seen in different political environments. For instance, Kavada (2020) discusses the role of a "hyperlocal infrastructure of care" in the emergence of mutual aid groups in response to Covid-19 in the UK. The discussion highlights how different tools (e.g., WhatsApp, Slack or Zoom) have different digital affordances that either enable or limit generativity. Kavada's analysis offers a comparison of the "decentralised organising model employed by mutual aid groups" and of the "more centralised NHS Volunteer Responders scheme." For instance, these models suggest different constructions of subjects. While hyperlocal mutual-aid projects rely on "equal and horizontal relationships of solidarity," the NHS volunteer scheme "makes a clearer distinction between those who are vulnerable – and registered formally as such by the state – and the volunteers who help them" (Kavada, 2020, online). In this light, this study can be considered as a starting point for a future comparative analysis of the link between Internet regulation and crisis-related resilience.

Conclusion

One may suggest that the link made here between empirical analysis of the role of digital platforms in response to Covid-19 in Russia and discussion of the role of Internet regulation in the context of global catastrophic risk is speculative. Indeed, this study does not attempt to suggest that we may reach some clear conclusion about the impact of regulation in the face of "the next catastrophe." That said, a juxtaposition of the mediational perspective and the notion of generativity enables us to expand our interpretative flexibility regarding the role of the Internet in the prevention and mitigation of global catastrophic risks (Avin et al., 2018). It highlights the meaning of the Internet as a resource for variability and preadaptation that should support new forms of humanity's leading activity (Ferholt et al., 2020) at a time of ever-growing uncertainty and existential risk. This framework highlights the ways in which Internet regulation, including sovereignization, may potentially restrict three critical aspects of addressing existential risk: how the risk is constructed as an object of activity, the scope of resources for addressing the risk, and how these resources can be mobilized.

This analysis of the Russian case demonstrates how Internet regulation changes the nature of the role of digital platforms in response to a crisis. Initially, digital platforms offer an opportunity for a broad range of crisis-related innovations and new forms of independent action. However, increasing control by the state in the digital domain achieves several goals. It limits the scope of digital innovation in a situation of crisis, restricts independent forms of crisis-related activities, and channels the mobilization of the digital crowd into state-sponsored channels. Although this type of regulation mitigates crisis-related political risks for the authorities, it also limits the social resilience of a society in the face of crisis.

To sum up, Internet regulation not only undermines the pace and potential of society's sociopolitical and cultural development, but also renders it more vulnerable to a variety of risks. The present analysis indicates that both users and state institutions stand to benefit from supporting the generativity of the Internet. The preservation of generativity is a key factor in securing the resilience of social and political systems in the face of crises yet to come. Conversely, the restriction of generativity would lead to a failure of the Internet as a system for the mitigation of catastrophic global risks, and to an increasing probability of failure to address existential threats.

Disclosure statement

No potential conflict of interest was reported by the author(s).

ORCID

Gregory Asmolov http://orcid.org/0000-0003-4744-1762

References

Agora International Human Rights Group. (2020). *The fake news 'infodemic': The fight against coronavirus as a threat to freedom of speech*. https://agora.legal/fs/a_delo2doc/196_file__ENG_final.pdf

Alexander, D. E. (2014). Social media in disaster risk reduction and crisis management. *Science and Engineering Ethics*, *20*(3), 717–733. doi:10.1007/s11948-013-9502-z

Asmolov, A. (1998). *Vygotsky today: On the verge of non-classical psychology*. Hauppauge, New York: Nova Science Publishers.

Asmolov, G. (2015). Vertical crowdsourcing in Russia: Balancing governance of crowds and state–citizen partnership in emergency situations. *Policy & Internet*, *7*(3), 292–318. doi:10.1002/poi3.96

Asmolov, G. (2018). The disconnective power of disinformation campaigns. *Journal of International Affairs*, *71*(1.5), 69–76.

Asmolov, G. (2019). The effects of participatory propaganda: From socialization to internalization of conflicts. *Journal of Design and Science*, *6*. https://jods.mitpress.mit.edu/pub/jyzg7j6x/release/2

Avin, S., Wintle, B. C., Weitzdörfer, J., Ó Héigeartaigh, S. S., Sutherland, W. J., & Rees, M. J. (2018). Classifying global catastrophic risks. *Futures*, *102*, 20–26. doi:10.1016/j.futures.2018.02.001

Barton, A. H. (1969). *Communities in disasters: A sociological analysis of collective stress situations*. New York: Doubleday, Anchor Books.

Beck, U. (2006). Living in the world risk society. *Economy and Society*, *35*(3), 329–345. doi:10.1080/03085140600844902

Benkler, Y. (2006). *The wealth of networks: How social production transforms markets and freedom*. New Haven, CT.: Yale University Press.

Bertrand, E. (2012). Constructing Russian power by communicating during disasters: The forest fires of 2010. *Problems of Post-Communism*, *59*(3), 31–40. doi:10.2753/PPC1075-8216590303

Bostrom, N. (2002). Existential risks – Analyzing human extinction scenarios and related hazards. *Journal of Evolution and Technology*, *9*(1), 1–30.

Bostrom, N., & Ćirković, M. M. (Eds.). (2008). *Global catastrophic risks*. Oxford: Oxford University Press.

Boyatzis, R. E. (1998). *Transforming qualitative information*. Thousand Oaks, CA.: Sage.

Coombs, W. T., & Holladay, S. J. (2004). Reasoned action in crisis communication: An attribution theory-based approach to crisis management. In D. P. Millar & R. Heath (Eds.), *Responding to crisis. A rhetorical approach to crisis communication* (pp. 95–115). Mahwah, NJ.: Erlbaum.

Cottle, S. (2006). Mediatized rituals: Beyond manufacturing consent. *Media, Culture and Society*, *28*(3), 411–432. doi:10.1177/0163443706062910

Couldry, N., & Hepp, A. (2017). *The mediated construction of reality*. Cambridge, UK: Polity Press.

Cuénot, L. (1914). Théorie de la préadaptation (The theory of preadaptation). *Scientia, 16*, 60–73.

Daucé, F., Loveluck, B., Ostromooukhova, B., & Zaytseva, A. (2020). From citizen investigators to cyber patrols: Volunteer Internet regulation in Russia. *Laboratorium: Russian Review of Social Research, 11*(3), 46–70.

Deibert, R., & Rohozinski, R. (2010). Control and subversion in Russian cyberspace. Access controlled: The shaping of power, rights, and rule in cyberspace. In R. Deibert et al. (Ed.), *Access controlled: The shaping of power, rights, and rule in cyberspace* (pp. 15-34). Cambridge, MA.: The MIT Press.

Diamond, L., & Plattner, M. (2010). Liberation technology. *Journal of Democracy, 21*(3), 69–83. doi:10.1353/jod.0.0190

Engeström, Y. (1988). How to do research on activity? *Quarterly Newsletter of the Laboratory of Comparative Human Cognition, 10*, 30–31.

Entman, R. (1993). Framing: Toward clarification of a fractured paradigm. *Journal of Communication, 43*(4), 51–58. doi:10.1111/j.1460-2466.1993.tb01304.x

Ermoshina, K., Loveluck, B., & Musiani, F. (2021). A market of black boxes: The political economy of internet surveillance and censorship in Russia. *Journal of Information Technology & Politics* (pp. 18-33).

Esser, F., & Matthes, J. (2013). Mediatization effects on political news, political actors, political decisions, and political audiences. In H. Kriesi, S. Lavanex, F. Esser, J. Matthes et al. (Eds.), *Democracy in the age of globalization and mediatization* (pp. 177–201). Basingstoke, UK: Palgrave Macmillan.

Ferholt, B., Guarrasi, I., Jornet, A., Nardi, B., Rajala, A., & Williams, J. (2020). Humanity's leading activity: Survival of the humanity of our species. *Mind, Culture, and Activity, 27*(2), 95–98. doi:10.1080/10749039.2020.1762654

Fink, S. (2002). *Crisis communication: Planning for the inevitable* (2nd ed.). New York: Amacom.

Freedom House. (2021). *Freedom on the Net 2021*. Freedomhouse.org, https://freedomhouse.org/article/new-report-global-battle-over-internet-regulation-has-major-implications-human-rights

Gonzalez-Herrero, A., & Pratt, C. B. (1996). An integrated symmetrical model for crisis communications management. *Journal of Public Relations Research, 8*(2), 79–105. doi:10.1207/s1532754xjprr0802_01

Gunitsky, S. (2015). Corrupting the cyber-commons: Social media as a tool of autocratic stability. *Perspectives on Politics, 13*(1), 42–54. doi:10.1017/S1537592714003120

Hepp, A. (2020). *Deep mediatization*. Abingdon, UK: Routledge.

Hoskins, A., & O'Loughlin, B. (2015). Arrested war: The third phase of mediatization. *Information, Communication & Society, 18*(11), 1320–1338. doi:10.1080/1369118X.2015.1068350

Johnston, L. (1996). What is vigilantism? *British Journal of Criminology, 36*(2), 220–236. doi:10.1093/oxfordjournals.bjc.a014083

Kaptelinin, V. (2014). The mediational perspective on digital technology: Understanding the interplay between technology, mind and action. In S. Price, C. Jewitt, & B. Brown (Eds.), *Sage handbook of digital technology research* (pp. 203–217). London: Sage.

Kaptelinin, V., & Nardi, B. A. (2006). *Acting with technology: Activity theory and interaction design*. Cambridge, MA.: The MIT Press.

Karanasios, S., Nardi, B., Spinuzzi, C., & Malaurent, J. (2021). Moving forward with activity theory in a digital world. *Mind, Culture, and Activity, 28*(3), 234–253. doi:10.1080/10749039.2021.1914662

Kavada, A. (2020, June 12). Creating a hyperlocal infrastructure of care: COVID-19 mutual aid groups. *OpenDemocracy*, https://www.opendemocracy.net/en/openmovements/creating-hyperlocal-infrastructure-care-covid-19-mutual-aid-groups/

Khanna, T., & Palepu, K. G. (2010). The nature of institutional voids in emerging markets. In T. Khanna & K. G. Palepu (Eds.), *Winning in emerging markets: A road map for strategy and execution* (pp. 13–26). Boston: Harvard Business Press.

Klyueva, A. (2016). Taming online political engagement in Russia: Disempowered publics, empowered state and challenges of the fully functioning society. *International Journal of Communication, 10*, 4661–4680.

Loveluck, B. (2019). The many shades of digital vigilantism: A typology of online self-jus-tice. *Global Crime* (pp. 213-241).

Mansell, R. (2012). *Imagining the internet: Communication, innovation, and governance*. Oxford: Oxford University Press.

Meier, P. (2015). *Digital humanitarians. How big data is changing the face of humanitarian response*. Milton Park, Abingdon-on-Thames: Taylor & Francis Press.

Mueller, M. (2017). *Will the Internet fragment? Sovereignty, globalization and cyberspace*. Cambridge, UK: Polity Press.

Musiani, F., Bronnikova, O., Daucé, F., Ermoshina, K., Ostromooukhova, B., & Zaytseva, A. (2021). The Russia "Sovereign Internet" facing COVID-19. In S. Milan, E. Treré, & S. Masiero (Eds.), *COVID-19 from the margins. Pandemic invisibilities, policies and resistance in the datafied society*. Amsterdam: Institute of Network Cultures (pp. 174-178).

Nambisan, S. (2017). Digital entrepreneurship: Toward a digital technology perspective of entrepreneurship. *Entrepreneurship Theory and Practice, 41*(6), 1029–1055. doi:10.1111/etap.12254

Palen, L., & Liu, S. B. (2007). Citizen communications in crisis: Anticipating a future of ICT supported public participation. *Proceedings of the SIGCHI Conference on Human Factors in Computing Systems*, San Jose, CA, April 28-May 3, (pp. 727–736).

Pelling, M., & Dill, K. (2006). 'Natural disasters' as catalysts of political action. *ISP/NSC Briefing Paper* 06/01, London: Chatham House, 4–6.

Perrow, C. (2011). *The next catastrophe: Reducing our vulnerabilities to natural, industrial, and terrorist disasters*. Princeton: Princeton University Press.

Rogers, M. B., & Pearce, J. M. (2016). The psychology of crisis communication. In A. Schwarz, M. W. Seeger, & C. Auer (Eds.), *The handbook of international crisis communication research* (pp. 34–44). Malden: John Wiley & Sons, Inc.

Samoilenko, S. (2016). Crisis management and communication research in Russia. In A. Schwarz, M. W. Seeger, & C. Auer (Eds.), *The handbook of international crisis commu-nication research* (pp. 397–410). Malden: John Wiley & Sons, Inc.

Sellnow, T., & Sellnow, D. (2010). The instructional dynamic of risk and crisis communication: Distinguishing instructional messages from dialogue. *The Review of Communication, 10*(2), 112–126. doi:10.1080/15358590903402200

Sivetc, L. (2021). Controlling free expression "by infrastructure" in the Russian internet: The consequences of RuNet sovereignization. *First Monday, 26*(5). https://firstmonday.org/ojs/index.php/fm/article/view/11698

Tierney, K. (2014). *The social roots of risk: Producing disasters, promoting resilience*. Stanford: Stanford University Press.

Vygotsky, L. S. (1978). *Mind in society: The development of higher psychological processes*. Cambridge, MA.: Harvard University Press.

Wijermars, M. (2021). Russia's law 'On news aggregators': Control the news feed, control the news? *Journalism, 22*(12), 1–17. doi:10.1177/1464884921990917

Zittrain, J. (2006). The generative internet. *119 Harvard Law Review, 1974*, 1974–2040.

Zittrain, J. (2008). *The future of the Internet and how to stop it.* New Haven Conn: Yale University Press.

Zuckerman, E. (2014). New media, new civics? *Policy & Internet, 6*(2), 151–168. doi:10.1002/1944-2866.POI360

Index

absolute proximity 48, 49
actors 2–4, 14, 94, 96, 99, 100, 105
additional bonds 75, 76, 78–81
affiliation 59, 64–67, 70, 71, 73–76, 78–81, 83–85; analysis 59, 64, 66; dialogic 65, 73–74; finessing 73
Anderson, B. 10
anti-conspiratorial comments 74, 79, 80, 82, 83
anti-elitist values 74–76, 79
attitude 65, 66, 68–73, 75, 77–82
audiences 2–4, 36, 38–41, 47, 48, 51, 68, 69, 73, 83; analyzing 41–42; reaction 41–43; reception 3, 35, 38, 42, 43
Avin, S. 91

Baudrillard, J. 39
Bolter, D. J. 41
bonds 64, 65, 70, 73–78, 81–83
Buzan, B. 11

Chouliaraki, L. 36, 47
communities 60, 61, 64, 66, 67, 69, 74, 83, 84, 90, 101, 103, 104
conspiracy theories 3, 58–62, 71, 76, 80, 84
conspiratorial comments 74–76, 78–81
conspiratorial discourse 3, 58–61, 83, 84
Covid-19 4, 11, 97–100, 102, 104–107
crisis-related activities 92, 107; systems 92, 95, 96, 105
crisis-related resilience 4, 89, 98, 107
crisis response 90, 92, 93, 98, 103, 105, 106
crisis situations 2, 3, 89, 90, 92, 93, 95, 96, 98, 100, 102, 105, 107

data analysis 45
dialogic affiliation 65, 73–74; strategies 74, 79
digital platforms 90–92, 94–98, 104–107; role of 90–92, 96–98, 105–107
distant refugee crisis 3, 35, 37, 53

electoral power 7, 8, 16, 17, 20, 23–25
elites 2, 75, 76
Entman, R. 92
existential threat 2, 6–8, 10–13, 19, 24, 25

Ferholt, B. 94
Finessing affiliation 71–73
France 61, 77
Fuchs, C. 62

Gamson, W. A. 14
generative system 95, 97
generativity 92, 94–97, 103–107
geographical distance 40
George, C. 23
Ginosar, A. 12
global catastrophic risks 91, 95, 97, 106, 107
Goffman, E. 14
Greece 2, 6–10, 12, 15, 16, 19–21, 23–25
Grusin, R. 41

Hoskins, A. 1
Huiberts, E. 41
humanitarian communication 35–39, 41–43, 50, 52, 53
human life, hierarchies of 40–41
hyperreality 39, 40, 46, 47

ideation 65, 66, 68–73, 75, 77–82
identity 10, 11, 19, 44
improper distance 37, 40, 47
independent projects 98, 103, 104
institutional actors 93, 96, 99, 100
intense spectacularity 37, 46
Internet 68, 69, 81, 82, 90, 91, 94, 95, 97, 99, 102, 106, 107
Internet regulation 4, 89–98, 102, 105–107; in crises 92–95; impact of 4, 91, 92, 95–97, 105; new forms of 97; role of 90–94, 97, 107
Irom, B. 51

Johnston, L. 102
Jones, S. 40

Kaptelinin, V. 94
Karanasios, S. 94
Kavada, A. 106
Kissas, A. 1

Kurasawa, F. 50
Kyriakidou, M. 42

legacy 2, 3, 19, 20
Lim, S. S. 60

Macedonia 2, 7, 10, 15, 18–21
Macedonian language 10, 20
Macedonian Name Dispute (MND) 6–10, 13, 15–17, 21–26
Mahl, D. 84
McRoberts, J. 38
mutual aid 101–104

Nardi, B. A. 94
Nash, K. 40, 41
nationalism 8, 10, 12, 24
nationalistic journalism 2, 6, 8, 10, 12, 24, 25
ND politician 18–20
news coverage 8, 13, 15, 22, 23, 25
news media 2, 7, 8, 13, 20–22, 24, 25, 41
news stories 13–16, 19–23, 25, 38
North Macedonia 6–8, 15–17, 19–22, 26

objects, regulation 99–100
O'Loughlin, B. 1
online platforms 2–4, 59

Pantti, M. 41
paradoxical cosmopolitan potential 39
participants 42–48, 50–52, 62; recruitment of 43–44
peace & international affair 21
de la Peña, N. 38
political & mobilization tools 16–17
Prespes Agreement 7, 8, 15, 16, 18–26
psychological distance 40
pure sentimentalism 50, 52

reality 39, 40, 45, 46, 51
refugees 3, 36, 46–48, 50, 79, 80
regulation: of subjects 100–103; of tools 103–105
research procedure 44

resilience 90–92, 94, 95, 97, 105, 107; development of 91, 92, 95, 97, 105
Russia 4, 9, 92, 97–99, 103–107

Schieferdecker, D. 42, 46
Scott, M. 41, 42
Seu, I. B. 42
Shin, D. 38
Silverstone, R. 48
Skopjan issue 15–17
social bonds 3, 61, 64, 66, 70, 71, 73, 74, 76, 83, 85
social constructionism 37
social values 60, 64, 83, 84
stimulus material 44
subject-object relationships 92, 95, 96
surveillance 100–102
symbolic construction 92, 93, 96
Syriza 7, 16, 17, 19, 20, 22, 24, 25
Systemic Functional Linguistics (SFL) 3, 59, 60; approach 59, 61, 84, 85
systemic functional linguistics approach 3, 58–85
Szenes, E. 84

territorial disputes 8–10, 14
Tierney, K. 90
Turkey 9, 19
tweets 61, 68, 72

ultimate empathy machine 3, 35, 36, 50, 53
user-crisis relationships 92, 95, 96, 98, 105, 106

values 3, 4, 13, 59, 60, 65–67, 69, 70, 74, 81–83, 106
venture 64, 70, 71
vertical crowdsourcing 98, 104, 105
virtual reality (VR) 3, 35–53

white supremacists 3, 58, 59, 61, 74, 83, 84
white supremacy 58–61, 84
World War 71, 72

YouTube 2, 3, 58–60, 62, 63, 71, 75
YouTuber 64, 66–71, 73, 74, 78, 79, 81–83